WRITTEN BY

RYAN SPRAGUE

SEASONS

WHAT COLLEGE ATHLETES NEED TO KNOW ABOUT THEIR FUTURE

FOREWORD BY MARK RICHT

4|| Communications

Tallahassee • Florida

SEASONS
What College Athletes Need to Know about Their Future

All marketing and publishing rights guaranteed to and reserved by:

4|| Communications

www.ryansprague.com

© 2013 Ryan Sprague

Cover by: James Barnett
Interior design by Erin Stark for TLC Graphics, *www.TLCGraphics.com*.

All rights reserved.

No part of this book may be reproduced in any manner whatsoever without written permission of 441 Communications, except in the case of brief quotations embodied in reviews.

ISBN: 978-0-9828763-2-9

Printed in the United States of America

STUDY AIDS / College Guides
REFERENCE / Personal & Practical Growth
SELF-HELP / Personal Growth / Success

*In honor of William "Grandpa" Murphy,
Paul "Grandpa" Sprague, Herman "Poppy" Borer
and Francis "Dzedo" Rudzik, four men whose legacy
is still at work in the lives of their great-grandchildren.*

CONTENTS

Acknowledgments	vii
Foreword by Mark Richt	xi
A Note to Students	xvii

CHAPTER ONE
Freedom: *Abuse It And Lose It* — 1

CHAPTER TWO
Media: *Controlling the Message* — 29

CHAPTER THREE
Money: *Scholarships and Spending* — 45

CHAPTER FOUR
Adversity: *Expect It and Attack It* — 63

CHAPTER FIVE
Relationships:
The Good Ones are Good, The Bad Ones are Bad — 77

SEASONS

CHAPTER SIX
    Identity: *Who You Are, Who You Aren't*   99

CHAPTER SEVEN
    Faith: *Asking the Right Questions*   117

CHAPTER EIGHT
    Coaches: *Trusting the Process*   137

CHAPTER NINE
    Decisions: *The Wise and The Fools*   155

CHAPTER TEN
    Leadership: *Can You Lead You?*   173

CHAPTER ELEVEN
    Opportunities: *Will You Be Ready?*   191

CHAPTER TWELVE
    Integrity: *Does Your Life Line Up?*   211

The Bench   233

About the Author   237

ACKNOWLEDGMENTS

THERE IS SOMETHING WONDERFUL about being part of a team. And even though writing is a mostly solitary effort, there was a fantastic team that helped make this book something to be proud of.

There are some specific people who were on the *Seasons* team who deserve a special thanks.

A big shoutout to the people who read *Seasons* back when it was called *Living Life, Playing Games* and offered their suggestions to make the book better: Jeni Sprague, Anthony Porterfield, Sam Lilly, Ross Brannon, Pat Wesolowski, Matt Wesolowski, Jerry Moore, Davis Moore, Mitch Murphy, and Kaitlyn Jaeger. You all did such a good job and provided the encouragement and corrections necessary to get this project done. Thank you!

Big thanks to Rebecca Barrack for offering to partner up on a future project and then actually returning my message when I called. I've never been so happy to see so much red ink. There is no denying you made

SEASONS

Seasons better than it was and provided some much needed peace of mind.

I was absolutely thrilled with the cover of this book and it's a credit to the creativity and vision of my longtime friend, James Barnett. Having never designed a book cover before, you even impressed the pros, and I'm so thankful you shared your talent with me on this project. I loved our time researching and brainstorming at the bookstore and hope we can do it again one day. And so it's forever in print ... I love you. ;)

Thanks to Tami Dever, Erin Stark, and the rest of the team at TLC Graphics (TLCGraphics.com) for making the interior of *Seasons* professional, sharp and appealing. I'm also appreciative for all the little extras you provided along the way. You guys did a great job!

I considered it a privilege to play for you, Coach Richt, and I'm honored that you were willing to attach your name to one of my projects. I appreciate you being one of those mentors in my life; your life's example was noticed and admired. Thanks for agreeing to do the foreword to *Seasons!*

Being a volume of wisdom, I'd be remiss if I didn't at least attempt to express my gratitude to all the men and women who have personally shared theirs with me over the years. In no particular order: Larry Sprague, Candi Sprague, Sam Lilly, Randy Hill, Dr. Bill Potts, John Lilly, Mark Richt, Bobby Bowden, Dave Van Halanger, Brian Tease, Clint Purvis, Jeni Sprague, Greg & Becky Rudzik, Bill McCutchen, Thomas Bates, Steve Kerhoulas, Phillip Coppage, Mark Meadows, Jim Cothran, Jay Drummonds, Clayton Lopez, Greg Boone, Curt

ACKNOWLEDGMENTS

Mackey, Ronnie Cottrell, Pat Wesolowski, Jay Miller, Tim Trask, Lee Hartsfield, Connie Moore, Dave Swanson, and Mark Mattfeld. I've no doubt forgotten someone and for that I'm deeply sorry, but know I'm very appreciative.

There are also a handful who've influenced me from a distance through their books: Randy Alcorn, Lou Holtz, Mike Krzyzewski, Max Lucado, Ravi Zacharias, Nancy Pearcey, John Piper, C.S. Lewis, G.K. Chesterton, Andy Stanley, Tony Dungy, John Wooden, Tim Keller, John Piper, John Maxwell, Ken Boa, Oswald Chambers, Gary Thomas, Bobby Bowden, Matthew, Mark, Luke, John, Paul, Peter, Moses, Solomon, James, Isaiah, and bundles of others who have books on my shelves.

I'm so grateful for my completely supportive family. Caedmon, Jackson, Andrew, Toby and Lucy, you guys are a constant source of motivation and joy to me personally and professionally. I often think of you as I write and think about writing. I hope you find encouragement and wisdom whenever you read your dad's books, and I especially hope you know how much I love you. And Jeni, my blossoming bride, you've fought through another series of beginnings, restarts, do-overs and "almost done's" to get *Seasons* finished. Many a late night and many more very early mornings where you loved on our kiddos so I could get my work done are recorded on the marital score card and the reward is a cruise, one of these days. I love you, I like you, and I'm looking forward to sitting on "The Bench" and watching the grandkids with you one day in our future.

SEASONS

And finally, all glory and honor belong to The Author, God, through Jesus Christ. I know I breathe because you created oxygen and lungs. I know I enjoy my sustenance because you created flavor and taste buds. I know I write because you inspire and give me the necessary capabilities to bring those ideas to the page. Thank you!

"For in him all things were created:
things in heaven and on earth, visible and invisible,
whether thrones or powers or rulers or authorities;
all things have been created through him and for him."

– COLOSSIANS 1:16

FOREWORD

I COACH FOOTBALL. When I first dreamed about coaching the game I loved, that's really all I imagined – coaching. The competition, the strategy, the X's and O's, conditioning, motivation and of course calling the plays. Just pure coaching. I also thought about the responsibility of helping boys grow into men, real men, most of them hoping to be husbands and fathers. They need to be able to excel at playing football and in life. Much of the job is still that, but today it's so much more.

Being a student-athlete in the early '80s was an entirely different experience than being one today. I was a part of some incredible teams and played with phenomenal athletes who became stars at the University of Miami and in the NFL. We had our share of trouble. As big as college football was, it was a shadow of what it is today in terms of exposure and national prominence. The entire landscape of college athletics has changed. For example, the year I enrolled at Miami – 1979 – is the same year a start-up television company

SEASONS

launched in Connecticut. Nobody had heard of ESPN when I was in school, but now that little concept is a worldwide corporation that's made sports, even college sports, a twenty-four hour a day reality.

Kids in South Florida weren't watching Oregon and Oregon State play football in the '80s. Most kids couldn't tell you their mascots, if they even knew the schools existed. Today you can watch those schools compete in all sports. College fans used to be primarily regional, and for the most part they still are, but now you'll find Wisconsin hats in Florida, Boise State shirts in Hattiesburg, Miss., Baylor Bear fans in New England, and Georgia Bulldogs in Paris. College athletics are now an international reality and the college athlete is an international player. Television changed everything.

If a college player at Miami got in trouble, one of the local writers might find out about it from scanning police reports the next day. Then an article might get printed in the local paper a day or two later. If it happened to be a really serious offense, the story might get picked up by other papers in the state, maybe around the south, but Texas A&M fans weren't reading about it in College Station. Now, if a student makes a mistake, it can be literally around the world in minutes and that young man or woman can move from a life of relative obscurity to national infamy overnight. Television brought scrutiny, but it also brought unheard of money.

Back in my day if there was a case where an athlete got paid people were able to operate under the radar and sneak cash to kids in various ways. If they were caught, they got in

FOREWORD

serious trouble. Schools lost their football programs. Now, because there is so much money involved, we're having a national debate about giving college athletes a salary. Furthermore, a freshman getting playing time was rare in my day. You had a few "once in a lifetime" guys, like Herschel Walker at Georgia, who were talented enough to make an impact in their first year, but they were the exception. Today's high school recruit comes in expecting to play immediately and just last year we awarded the Heisman to a freshman for the first time in history.

The rapid changes in college athletics have had an earthquake-like effect on the student athlete's foundation. Today's athlete has to be able to handle intense public scrutiny while they're still teenagers. They are often asked to speak on the great social concerns of our time even though they are still getting lost trying to find their classes. The college experience used to be about savoring the best times of your life and it still can be, but first they must learn to navigate these challenges.

These challenges are why this book so important. It deals with issues today's student athlete must address but it does so in a way that attracts the attention of the student-athletes. By using the conversational setting, *Seasons* is able to convey timeless wisdom without ever lecturing. Bringing all the different characters into the story allows this book to connect with students of all different backgrounds where the singular voice of one communicator might struggle to create the same resonance. Today's student athlete wants to have a voice, to be a part of the conversation. *Seasons* gives them that opportunity, while at the same time it providing enough structure to lead them where they need to go and get them talking about all the elephants crowding the room. In that sense, it's a lot like coaching because a good coach has to get players to do the things they may not want to do in order to lead them to where they want to go. This book is a good coach.

I met Ryan Sprague when he walked-on to the Florida State football team back in 1996. I was the Offensive Coordinator at the time. He paid his dues on the scout team for a couple years, earned a scholarship, and then bounced between three positions while the coaches tried to figure out where he might be able to fit. He wasn't big enough to play on the line, but wasn't really athletic enough to play his natural position of tight end, and was far too tall at 6'5" to play fullback, yet he played all three before maturing into the starting tight end for our National Championship team in 1999.

His personal experience as both a walk-on and a scholarship athlete – a fifth-stringer and a starter – gives him the unique capacity to speak to athletes across the board. Our team experienced great success – an undefeated National Championship season – yet we also fought through very public challenges – our Heisman candidate being suspended for getting in legal trouble. So Ryan has a "been there" set of experiences that garners him great credibility with today's college athlete. Now he's been married for over a decade, is the father of five children, and after a brief stint in the NFL was able to "go pro in something other than sports" both as an author and working in the non-profit world, giving him the

FOREWORD

benefit of perspective. These realities are all evident in *Seasons* giving it both a relatable authenticity and a reliable authority that I've never seen in a book for student athletes before.

The reality for the student athlete has certainly changed. The scope of responsibilities for the college coach has changed as well. Coaches face on-the-field pressures like never before while also being expected to help young men and women mature into upstanding citizens under a glaring spotlight. It's a very difficult task at best, which is why I'm so appreciative for what Ryan has done with this book. His goal is to help coaches by providing a resource that will help the student athlete become a better player as they become better people.

– MARK RICHT, 2013

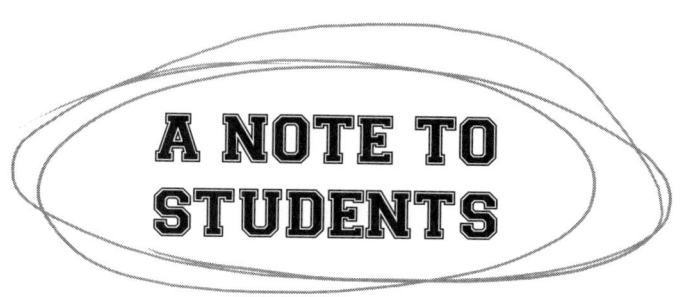

A NOTE TO STUDENTS

THIS BOOK IS DIFFERENT, a bit of an illusion. You picked it up, perhaps, because you were intrigued by the title and have college on your mind. If you found it in a bookstore, you might have been looking at college prep guides or self-help books and found yourself holding this. But if you were to start reading the book you might find the style surprising, maybe even confusing. One of the people I asked to review *Seasons* when it was still in draft form had this to say,

> "As I started to read I realized that your writing was totally not what I expected. The typical book for a college bound student consists of chapters: 'financial aid,' 'dorm life,' 'class selection,' 'party life,' etc. Your narrative is very unique and interesting. I found myself getting a little lost with the first few chapters. I didn't understand what you were trying to relate to the reader. But finally my old mind and ways began to kick in. This wasn't the typical book I looked at back in the '60s. This

SEASONS

book is thought provoking. I turned back to the first page and started again."

Like I said, *Seasons* is different. I envisioned you sitting through lectures all day, carrying around a stack of textbooks and assigned reading, then listening to directions from your coach and realized another "typical book" might look nice on the shelf, but you probably wouldn't read it. So, I set out to write a book full of helpful information that you would actually enjoy reading. The literary world calls this genre of book creative non-fiction. "Ultimately, the primary goal of the creative nonfiction writer is to communicate information, just like a reporter, but to shape it in a way that reads like fiction." The previous statement was made by a writer named Leo Gutkind, and it perfectly describes why I made *Seasons* different. Instead of chapters such as "financial aid," "dorm life," "class selection," "party life," etc., I chose to wrap the information in a story, and *Seasons* was born.

    The main character is a young man named J Foxe who is about to go to college on an athletic scholarship. That's all you need to know about J for now, but I do want you to know he was created with you in mind. His purpose is to give you a voice. I believe the ideas in this book are important for you to think about and apply to your life, but you need to own them if they are going to make a difference. You need to wrestle with them and test their strength. I tried to imagine how you might react to the advice being offered and allowed J to do just that. As you read, I hope you find yourself agreeing with J when he asks questions and find satisfaction with how his questions

A NOTE TO STUDENTS

are answered. He won't say everything you're thinking and you might even disagree with him, and that's great. I just hope you'll talk about your ideas with somebody, which is why I added the discussion questions. There are a few questions following every chapter and I hope you find them helpful as you think about the ideas in this book.

I remember my days playing football at Florida State. I remember mistakes and I remember conversations with people of wisdom who helped me navigate those rough seas. Since my time in college, things have only grown more complicated which leaves you trying to find your way in far tougher circumstances than I experienced. That's why *Seasons* exists. Hopefully the advice in this book will help you avoid some of the traps that have caught so many. And hopefully these ideas will help you to thrive while you're in college. And when this season of your life is done, I want you to know authentic, healthy success through all the remaining seasons. I hope you enjoy *Seasons* and I truly wish you only God's best!

– RYAN

P.S.: There is a poem at the end of this book called *The Bench*. It was inspired by the picture on this book's cover and is just a little something extra. I hope it speaks to you.

*There are three kinds of men.
The ones that learn by readin'.
The few who learn by observation.
The rest of them have to pee on the
electric fence for themselves.*
– WILL ROGERS, actor and comedian

*I know I have a son who doesn't listen
to anything I say and if he hears the same thing
from someone else, sometimes it has a little more impact.*
– TONY DUNGY, two-time Super Bowl-winning coach

– chapter one –

ABUSE IT AND LOSE IT

*While we are free to choose our actions,
we are not free to choose
the consequences of our actions.*
– STEVEN R. COVEY, author and businessman

*Freedom consists not in doing what we like,
but in having the right to do what we ought.*
– JOHN PAUL II, 264th Pope of the Roman Catholic Church

SEASONS

I USED TO LIVE FOR FRIDAY NIGHTS. Years before I ever put on a uniform I'd go over to Shaw Field for Cougars games, but I never watched from the bleachers. Bleachers are for the band, or fans, or parents, but players belong on the field and because I knew I would wear the green and gold one day, the field was where I stood. And I didn't just watch the games, I dissected them. Don't get me wrong, I was the biggest fan in Shaw, but I was a student of the game first. I knew the players' warm-up routine by heart and when Tyler, my younger brother, was old enough, I taught him so we could play pretend games in our backyard. By the time I graduated the eighth grade, the tension on my life's sling shot was at its peak, and I launched into Columbia County High School on a mission.

That was four years ago now. I can still hear the band echoing in my head and I remember plays like I just finished making them, but Fridays are behind me. Now I live for Saturdays. A couple hundred fans are being replaced with tens of thousands. The Cougars' green and gold is being traded for the silver and red of State where I got a scholarship to play middle linebacker.

This particular Saturday, I was long into a dream that included me running toward the end zone after an interception. Just as I was about to score, I was blasted from my left and knocked out of bounds.

"Mom said you have to get up." It was Tyler, and it was before 8:00 AM. I wasn't planning to see either on this particular Saturday, but when I heard the alarm on my iPhone I remembered I was supposed to be up at 7:30.

FREEDOM

Pulling back my covers, Tyler said, "C'mon, J, Mom said Grandpa's gonna be here any minute." She's not technically my mom, but to him she is. My biological mother died when our house burned down. I was two. A couple years after the fire, my dad met Mary and they got married. She's the real mom of my two little brothers and she's now "mom" to me, too. The truth is I don't really remember my mom, but I keep a picture of her in my room and Dad tells me about her sometimes.

The old house was out in the country, closer to my high school. But after the fire, we went to live with my grandparents and that's where Dad met Mary. They didn't date very long before they were married. She had a house in the city — this house — so after the wedding we moved in with her. Being in the city limits, I was supposed to go to Lincoln High, but since my dad teaches history out at Columbia County I was allowed to go there. It worked out great for me. There are too many schools in the city and the good athletes are spread out all over town. And they don't care about football the way the people out in Columbia County do. People still go to the games but it's different in the county. There's just the one school and since most everybody who lives there went there, they love the Cougars, especially on Friday nights. It doesn't hurt that the Cougars are the best program in the northern half of the state. They've won seven state championships and I helped them win two.

I smacked Tyler with my pillow and sat up on the side of my bed. The soundtrack music from *300* was still playing through my iPhone so I grabbed it to turn it off. It was 8:28 AM; my grandpa would be here to pick me up in two minutes and the old man is never late. As I got out of bed I hit Tyler with another pillow, "Thanks Ty, don't ever do it again." I ran for the closet, but there was a pair of black workout shorts on the floor that looked clean, so I pulled them on. I grabbed an old Cougars "State Champs" T-shirt, a pair of slides and ran down stairs. Mom had pancakes and bacon on the table, but there was no time so I grabbed a Pop-Tart from the pantry on my way out. Tyler had a plate full of pancakes and a mouth full of bacon, which made me jealous. My baby brother was playing with some Cheerios and had milk dripping down the side of his face from the cereal bowl on his head, which didn't make me jealous at all. Mom was pretending it hadn't happened so she could enjoy her coffee in peace. I kissed her on the cheek and made for the door, "Bye, Mom, I'll text you later."

I might have slept in, but it felt like the sun had been up for hours. Sweat was forming on my forehead by the time I walked down my back sidewalk to the drive, and when I turned the corner, the air directly above the road was already blurred from the heat radiating off the asphalt. I grew up in this oven we call a state, but I still wasn't used to it. Plenty of people swear they're used to it, some even claim to like it, but I think they're all suffering from some form of heat-related delusion. The only beings on the planet that could possibly like this are the gnats. Miserable creatures. But I even wonder about them because the first thing they do is

FREEDOM

swarm to my body like they're doing right now, and I think they're just trying to dip their little gnat feet in the gnat-sized pools of sweat beading down my arms. Hot is just gross, but hot is where I live.

I heard my grandpa's old truck before I saw it. It had an engine only a masochistic mechanic could love and a color only my grandpa could. He loves burnt orange; I've never understood why he loves that color, but he's always been a little OCD about it. If you're paying attention, you'll notice it everywhere he spends any time. And because he would spend time in his truck, he wanted it to be that dirty orangish shade he so admires. The only problem was nobody offered it as a color option from the factory, so he got his hands on an old beater and literally hand painted it. With a brush. The heat got to him a long time ago. No lie, he went to Lowe's with a sweat-stained Texas Longhorns hat and had the paint guy match it. The truck had the same kind of paint I had in my room, just uglier. But he loved it and it was to be my ride today. Just add it to my list of complaints about the morning.

I shoved the last half of the first brown sugar and cinnamon Pop-Tart in my mouth as he rumbled around the corner. The horrible paint job is enough to make his truck one of a kind, but there are two other features that make it unmistakably grandpa's: The license plate that said "SWAPD," and his old English bulldog, Henry, riding shotgun. The guys out in the county called my grandpa Swap because he'd always been tight with his money and would rather trade than spend a dime. The truck was his proudest deal. He exchanged a lawn

SEASONS

mower, a spare TV, and a baseball autographed by Hank Aaron to get it, and he even got the previous owner to throw in twenty dollars cash for the truck's new paint. Grandpa loved the trade because none of the stuff he traded mattered to him in the least. He hadn't used the lawn mower in years because my cousin, Scott, handled his yard care. That TV only existed for us to watch cartoons when we were kids. Grandpa never turned it on; he was a reader. He knows Hank Aaron personally and had the ball replaced before the paint on the truck had time to dry. He was a crafty old man, but he always said, "That's how tradin' goes," and he loved it.

He rolled to a stop in front of our house at exactly 8:30 AM. I grabbed the handle and as I creaked the door open, my phone went off. I stepped onto the runner and tried to get in the truck, but Henry wouldn't budge. "Get out of the way Slobber! Lazy old dog." Grandpa grabbed his collar and dragged him to the middle of the bench so I could climb in. He tried to sound tough, but he loved that dog. My grandma found him at the pound when he was a puppy and brought him home as a form of revenge with fleas. Grandma wanted to name my dad Henry, but Grandpa insisted that his son would carry on the family name. Grandpa didn't like the name Henry and Grandma never really got over it, so after their kids were out of the house she found the dog and named him Henry before my grandpa had a chance to object. But, true to form, he wouldn't be budged, and refused to call him by his actual name; he always called the dog Slobber. It drove Grandma crazy, and Grandpa loved it. She passed away

FREEDOM

the summer before I started high school and the old dog has been at my grandpa's side ever since.

Dust puffed out from the old seat when I sat on it. I went to check my phone, but Henry smelled my breakfast and lunged for it. I dropped my phone, but managed to keep his slobbery face away from my Pop-Tart. "Slobber!" Grandpa grabbed him by his neck skin and jerked the old dog into his lap. I leaned down and picked up my phone, closed the door, and the truck started rolling. The text was from my mom, *"Justin, make sure you listen to your grandfather, and don't forget to pick up the milk on your way home."* She was the only person in town who called me Justin. Most people didn't even know it was my real name, and almost no one knew it was my grandpa's name too. He was Justin Samuel Foxe, just like my dad and just like me. People knew my dad as Sam, or Coach, and everybody called me "J." People just assume my name's J-A-Y, Jay, so they don't even know it's a nickname. Mom preferred Justin, so that's what she called me and Dad; she's old school. But even she calls my grandpa Swap.

She's starting to get sad about me leaving for college, so for the last few months she's been saying things that she hasn't said to me since I was eight or nine years old, like "listen to your grandfather." When she bought party hats for my 18th birthday I knew something was up. Then I found her watching all our old home videos and I knew she was not going to take my move well. She's cried more recently than she's ever cried before and it happens at the strangest times. Just last week we were walking through Wal-Mart and without warning she stopped in the aisle and began sobbing. I turned to see what had happened and she was staring at the little boys clothing section, whimpering something about how she used to buy my shirts there. I just laughed, took a picture and sent it to my dad. She was a wreck at graduation and I can't imagine what moving day is gonna be like, but I know there will be serious tears.

"Hey, Grandpa. Hey, Henry," I finally said.

"Morning, J. You ready for today?" he asked.

"I guess, but I've got no idea what we're doing. What are we doing?"

"I'm taking you to the shop with me. I've got some people I'd like you to meet." Grandpa had a twinkle in his eye and a hint of mischief in his tone.

"That's cool. Can I get a cut while we're there?"

"My treat."

It was always his treat. In fact, I'd never known any Foxe to pay for a hair cut. I gave Henry a piece of my Pop-Tart and finished the rest. For the rest of the ride out of town I just stared out the window and scratched Henry's ears. Grandpa still lived out in Columbia County, just up the road from where our old house was. We drove about twenty minutes before we passed my high school. The parking lot was almost empty. The sign on the road said, "Home of the Cougars" in hunter green and Vegas gold. Just under that, the marquee said, "Enjoy your summer." Finally, the bottom of the sign read, "Back-to-Back State Champions," and it made me smile every time I saw it. I was the starting fullback and a good one,

FREEDOM

but middle linebacker was my best position. I'd made first team all-state and was offered a scholarship to play defense in college. A few schools wanted me to play fullback, but I stopped talking to them quickly. In spite of all the state championships, I was the first Columbia County player to get a Division-I football scholarship. Cougar football teams were always full of what my dad called "scrappers." None of them were ever big enough to go D-I, but quite a few had played D-II ball. We'd had plenty of guys earn baseball scholarships, and most of them stayed in town to play at the local school. It was too small to field a football team, but its baseball team was in the NCAA postseason almost every year. Grandpa was a legend at Spalding College. He still owned most of the hitting records, but he tore his shoulder up after his senior season and never played again. The legend says he traded all his baseball equipment to the owner of the hardware store for a new barber's kit, talked the bank into giving him a loan to rent a little shop on Sixth Avenue, and opened up "Swap's Shop" that summer. He talked the college kids into trading free haircuts for mercy while he taught himself the barber's craft. But it wasn't long before he was the best in town and Swap's Shop has been thriving ever since.

He owned the building now, and it was perfectly maintained. Grandpa painted the little shop every other year and kept it as clean as any hospital. It looked like a tiny house, complete with a little front porch and two rocking chairs. The screen door was the only splash of color against the white building. He'd painted it with his trademark burnt orange.

SEASONS

The screen was closed, but the front door was open because my uncle was already there. Jeff had married into the family back in the '80s and lost his job about ten years ago. Grandpa brought him on to run the business side of things and trained him to become a barber himself.

Henry was on his feet with his nub tail wiggling like a worm on a hook when we pulled up to the curb. As soon as Grandpa opened the door, the lumpy old dog ran for the shop. His back feet slipped out from under him as he went up the curb, but he kept on moving. He pawed at the screen a few times before he caught it and pushed it open just wide enough for his fat, wrinkled body to squeeze through. Grandpa and I followed, and by the time we were inside Henry was laying spread eagle on the tile floor with his tongue hanging out the side of his mouth.

"Morning, Swap. How you doing, J?"

"Good morning, Jeff." My grandpa grabbed the paper and sat in one of the big barber chairs.

"I hear you're going to be spending the day with us, J."

"You know more than I do. I didn't know I was coming to the shop till Grandpa picked me up. All I know is he wants me to meet some people."

Henry got up, walked in a few circles and dropped right back down while Jeff finished getting the store ready to open and Grandpa commented on the baseball scores.

"Jeff, Swap said I could get a cut. When you get ready will you set me up?"

FREEDOM

"Sure. Jump in the other chair and I'll be with you in a minute."

Swap's Shop has always been popular with the college kids and Grandpa loved talking with them while he cut their hair. A mirror spanned the wall in front of me, but most of it was covered with schedule posters from all the different teams at the university. Directly in front of the chairs, so people could actually watch while they were getting trimmed, are little oval-shaped breaks in the picture mosaic so the mirror could do its job. Above the mirror, and surrounding the little shop, autographs and notes from the customers adorned the walls. Behind my grandfather's chair was a picture of him and Hank Aaron which had been autographed, "*Swap, thanks for the cut, best trade I ever made! Hank Aaron, #44.*" Right below that was a picture of my grandpa in front of an old brown truck with Henry at his feet and a man holding a TV that my grandpa inscribed, "*best trade I ever made!*"

Jeff turned on the local talk radio station, snapped a white barber's cloth around me and began cutting my hair when a man walked into the shop. "Bobby!" Swap stood and embraced the man who had just entered the shop. He was just over six feet tall with emerald green eyes that contrasted his deeply suntanned skin. I'm guessing he was in his thirties. The long sleeves of his green shirt were rolled up past his elbows. "First Step Expeditions" was embroidered on the left pocket in chocolate brown. The shirt was tucked into a pair of brown cargo shorts, threaded by a navy blue belt that was made from braided nylon rope. His acorn brown and black hiking boots were low cut and had burnt orange striping crisscrossing the sides.

"It's been way too long, Swap. Good to see you."

"How long has it been?"

"The last time I was home was for Chad Dyer's wedding. It's been at least five years now."

"And now your little sister's getting married. I'm getting old, Bobby."

"Yeah, well me too. I remember changing Annie's diapers and now she's gettin' hitched."

Swap smiled and shook his head. "Any news on the marriage front for you?"

"Not yet, but Mom's been harassing me about it since I got in town. She's convinced I'll never meet anyone in Peru."

"She's probably more concerned you will, and then her grand-babies will live below the equator and she'll never see them."

"You may be on to something there, Swap. This must be the grand-baby you've been telling me about." The man walked over to me and extended his hand. "The name's Robert Earle, but, as you probably heard, everyone calls me Bobby. You're J, right?"

I stood and clasped Bobby's hand. "Yessir, I'm the grand-baby." Bobby laughed.

Jeff raised his left eyebrow, "Grand-baby moose, maybe."

"Good old Jeff. It's nice to see you haven't changed; still almost funny." He and Jeff shook hands, smiling.

"Maybe so, but smarter and better looking than you'll ever be."

FREEDOM

They converted their handshake into a hug. "It's great to see you, Jeff. Pretty as a prom dress."

"At least I had a date to the prom."

"I don't think I'd count your sister as a date there, Jeff." I laughed. Bobby continued, "Besides, somebody had to save the world." He walked across the room and sat in Swap's chair.

"Can I give you a trim while you talk, Bobby?" Swap said.

"Actually, that would be fantastic."

Swap wrapped the barber cloth around Bobby's neck and grabbed his scissors.

"Wait," I looked over at Jeff, "did you really take your sister to the prom?"

"She was doing me a favor. Besides, the prom's a ridiculous waste of time. Aren't you supposed to be talking to Bobby?"

"You didn't marry her did you?" I asked.

"You see what you've started, Bobby?" Jeff shook his head.

"Hey, it's what I do," Bobby said.

"What do you do, Bobby?" I asked.

He pointed to the logo on his shirt, "I run First Step Expeditions."

"Wait, wait, wait." Swap held his scissors up in the air. "Before we get too far, let me tell you what's going on, J."

"I'd appreciate that. What is going on?"

"I asked Bobby to come by and talk with you today."

"Okay. About what?"

"I'll let him tell you that. But he's just the first. I've invited quite a few people to come by the shop today and talk with you."

SEASONS

"Should I be worried?"

My grandfather smiled. "No. You've no need to worry. I'm hoping you'll actually enjoy yourself. You're going to meet some pretty incredible people."

"But why?"

"Well, I thought it would be good for you to hear from some people who've already been where you're about to go."

"Swap, I'm not planning on going to Peru."

"Like I said, I'll let Bobby tell you his story."

"Okay." I looked at Bobby through the mirror while Swap went back to work with his scissors. "So what is First Step Expeditions?"

"It's the company I started. I lead survival trips through the Amazon River Basin and the Andes Mountains."

"Like Bear Grylls?"

"Kinda like that but without the gross. I don't eat bugs. Bear's much more extreme than I am. Most of the people I take out just want to see monkeys, but also want to tell their friends they went on a survival adventure. We eat protein bars."

"Have any cool stories?"

"Tons of 'em. But my customers' favorite is about the time I was leading a father and son through the jungle and I got up close and personal with a caiman."

"What's a caiman?"

"It's a close cousin to gators and crocodiles, but the caiman isn't the best part. We'd set up camp and I slipped a few feet down a bank. No big deal. But when I got up on one knee there was a six-foot caiman from me to you hissing. I froze.

FREEDOM

Generally they won't mess with you, but I'd spooked this guy and he wasn't happy. I was figuring out what to do next, and I'm talking about seconds here, when a huge jaguar leaped from the brush. The cat laid into that caiman's throat while the lizard thrashed. I couldn't help but watch for a second, but I came to my senses and got out of there while I still had my life. It was by far the most incredible thing I've seen and scariest."

"But what did you do after that? Did you still camp there?"

"Yeah. The caiman was eventually dead and the jaguar wasn't hungry anymore."

"Are you serious?"

"J, the Amazon is full of animals that could kill you. Moving camp a few hundred yards wouldn't all of a sudden make it safer. And the big animals are the least of your problems. Including my rescuer, I've only seen three jaguars in all my years leading First Step. It's all the little ones, like bugs, frogs and snakes, that'll get ya."

"That's just a little bit terrifying."

"That's what makes it so exciting."

"With all that danger and adventure why did you name your company First Step?"

"An old Chinese proverb I like says, 'A journey of a thousand miles begins with a single step.' I borrowed the idea to make F.S.E. Our slogan is, 'The adventure of a lifetime begins with the first step.' Pretty catchy, don't you think?"

"I'm ready to go," Jeff said.

SEASONS

"Come on down to Peru. I'll lead you myself, but I might make you eat a few beetles."

"Maybe next summer. But what does Amazon survival have to do with playing college ball?" I asked.

"Nothing really," Bobby said, "but my job and your freshman year have one thing in common: Survival."

"Survival?"

"Survival. But, before I get in to all that, let me tell you a little of my story. I was a linebacker in high school and went on to the Naval Academy in Annapolis. I wanted to be a Navy Seal."

"Why weren't you?"

"In the third quarter of the Notre Dame game, in my senior season, I tore my knee up bad — ACL and MCL. I missed the rest of the year, but that's not what hurt. The real pain began when they told me I was medically disqualified from becoming a SEAL. I was heartbroken. Long story short, I was assigned to an intelligence gig, served five years and then retired from the service. The intelligence stuff was interesting, but I couldn't stand being indoors all day. I've always been intrigued by the Amazon, so I relocated to Peru and started First Step."

"Had you ever been to the Amazon?" I asked.

"Nope. But I'd never been to Annapolis either. Didn't stop me then, so I figured it wasn't a good excuse for Peru."

"Has anyone ever said you're a little crazy?"

"My mom was the first one, but it's no crazier than you wanting to play pro ball. Shoot, your career's probably more

FREEDOM

dangerous; there's no chance of being run over by a truck in a rain forest."

"Well, I'll be the one running people over, so you won't have to worry about me."

"I hear ya big shot, but come talk to me after you meet one of those three hundren ten-pound diesels that make a living out of trucking pip squeak linebackers like yourself."

"They can't hit what they can't catch."

"Confidence can be a good thing, J, but in the Amazon, over-confidence can get you killed. If you want to survive in the rain forest, you have to respect what you're up against. And the same's true of college, believe it or not."

"How so?"

"The most difficult person for me to lead on an expedition is the guy who read a book about survival and thinks he's an expert. Inevitably, Mr. Big Shot will eat a poisonous plant and end up puking for two days. The other tough customer is on the other end of the bridge. We call 'em PFO's — Panicked, Freaking Out."

"That would be Jeff," I said.

"You're probably right," Bobby said, smiling.

"I'm standing right here guys. I can hear you. And I'm holding the scissors, J."

Swap moved around to the left side of Bobby and kept clipping his hair.

"J, the problem is the same for both people – more freedom than they can handle."

SEASONS

"What's eating a poisonous plant or being a PFO got to do with freedom?"

"We take a chopper to the starting point for our expeditions, a little plateau a few thousand feet above the canopy of the forest that provides access to the Andes and to the jungle. When the chopper leaves, the adventure begins, and the adventure begins with a choice: Up or down. We always come prepared for a mountain expedition or a jungle adventure and let the client decide on the plateau. The PFO's freeze and the Big Shot's start climbing the peaks in shorts and a T-shirt."

"I'd go for the jungle," I said.

"Okay, perfect, jungle it is. Before we go down, we talk about First Step."

"Your company?"

"First Step is more than the name of my company. It's also a mnemonic for survival. S.T.E.P. stands for Stay calm, Take inventory, Establish a plan, and Put one foot in front of the other. They're the four simple steps I use to survive, and they apply to the freshman college student as well."

"How's that?"

"The first mistake my customers make is losing their cool. The Big Shot lets his brain fall out and his bravado lead him, while the PFO lets his brain fall out and his emotions lead him. Neither will make it."

"I can see that, but what does it have to do with college?"

"Everything. Most college kids, especially athletes, fall into the Big Shot category. They arrive at school, unpack their brains with their suitcase and let bravado lead the way. There's

FREEDOM

nothing wise about keg stands, one-night stands, or drug use. It's all showmanship; people trying to one up each other. Just a bunch of egos in a room looking to impress. Mom and dad are a few hundred miles away, so they have more freedom than they've ever had before, and they start climbing in their T-shirts, if you know what I'm saying."

"So the problem is freedom?"

"Not at all. The problem isn't freedom; freedom is beautiful. The problem is their abuse of freedom. One of my old coaches used to say, 'Abuse leads to restriction' and he was exactly right. The quickest way to lose your freedom is to abuse your freedom."

"So, you're saying I shouldn't drink and do drugs. I already know all that."

"That's not what I'm saying. I'm telling you to stay calm. I force our groups to remain on the plateau for at least an hour before we do anything. If for nothing else, it helps them calm down. It's natural to be excited and eager to get started, but it's my job to help them stay calm. We talk about the scenery, I'll ask them what they're thinking they want to do, and I try to help them get their bearings before we start. You should do the same thing when you get to school. You're gonna be excited; every freshman is. Just give yourself some time to learn where your classes are, make a few friends, figure out how much time your studies will take. That's part two of the S.T.E.P. plan. Take inventory."

"Inventory of what?"

SEASONS

"If you were on my plateau and saw a wicked storm headed for the peaks, you'd probably be inclined to head for the jungle. On the other hand, if you got spooked by a howler monkey, you might opt for the mountains. It's part of taking inventory – evaluate what you have to work with and where you want to go. Not everybody can do everything the same you know."

"So what does it mean for me?"

"Let me give you an example. I struggled in school; learning never came easy for me. I did well, but it required me to work hard. I had friends who seemed to breeze through. They'd be out running around after school, but I'd only be half finished with my homework. I could have joined them in the street, but I wanted to go to the Naval Academy so I finished my work. I knew where I wanted to go, and I also knew I would have to bust it to get there. I took inventory. Jump back over to my plateau; only a fool would opt for the Andes trip and neglect to tell me he's got asthma. You see what I mean? It's not that someone with asthma cannot make the trip, but we have to pace it differently."

"So taking inventory means understanding my abilities, limitations and available resources," I said.

"That's it, but don't forget about deciding where you want to go. Your desired destination determines what you do with the third step."

"Which is?"

"E. Establish a plan."

FREEDOM

Swap finished with the scissors and started using the buzzers. I had to speak up so Bobby could hear me over my grandpa's work.

"Isn't that the same as deciding where I want to go?"

"Hardly," Bobby said. "Deciding *where* you want to go is a small part of it. Establishing a plan is about *how* you'll get there. Even more, it's about how to avoid ending up where you *don't* want to be."

"Wouldn't that happen automatically?" I said. "I mean, if I plan to go to Chicago, wouldn't that mean I'd avoid Los Angeles?"

"Yes, it should mean that. But there's more to it than just getting to your destination. Establishing a plan also deals with your condition when you arrive."

"My condition?"

"Yeah. On my expeditions, everyone wants to get back to the base camp. Some go up, some go down, but they all want to get to base."

"Okay."

"My next question messes up the PFO's pretty bad. I'll ask them, 'Do you want to get there on your feet or on a gurney?'"

"That would mess me up," Jeff said.

"Why would you ask that?" I asked.

"Because it affects the plan."

"Why would that affect the plan?"

"Because if they're content to arrive on a gurney it saves me a lot of planning. However, if they want to arrive healthy, on their feet, we have to plan for it."

"I still think that would be assumed."

"That's the Big Shot in you. As soon as you assume in the Amazon, you pick up a pretty frog and end up terribly sick, and, in extreme cases, dead. A dead man arrives at base camp, just like he wanted, but he arrives on a gurney. If you want to arrive on your feet, you will follow my guidelines."

"That makes sense for the jungle, but there's no poison dart frogs on a college campus."

"No. But there's plenty of poison: alcohol, drugs, STD's, et cetera."

"Then you are telling me not to drink and stuff."

"Not exactly. The law says you can't drink until you're twenty-one and can't ever smoke marijuana. In your experience, do students fear the law?"

"No, people do that stuff all the time."

"Exactly," Bobby pressed further. "Do their parents let them do it?"

"A few do, but most of them don't."

"So, even though their parents and the law says they can't drink, some still do?"

"Most still do, actually."

"Do you think being away at college will change their behavior?"

"They'll probably do it more."

Bobby got a twinkle in his eye. "Why do you think that is?"

"Because they don't have to worry about their parents catching them."

"Exactly."

FREEDOM

"So what?"

"This is why it doesn't matter if I tell you not to drink. I won't be at your college watching your every move. You'll have the freedom to do as you wish. The only thing that will keep you from the poisons is the condition you want to be in when you reach your destination. If you want to just be on the team and graduate, you'll find yourself at plenty of parties. But, if you want to be your best athletically and academically, you'll choose differently."

"I get that, but where does the plan come in?"

"The plan involves where you *won't* go, just as much as where you *will* go. What you *won't* do, as much as what you *will* do. It determines your line of surrender."

"My line of surrender?"

"If you want to survive, you have to have one. It doesn't mean to quit; it means you'll find another way, or simply be patient. You might need to cross a river to get to base camp, but not if there's a dozen hungry crocodiles looking for dinner, or a category five rapid tearing through the gorge. That's your line of surrender. You're surrendering your ego, goals and plans to the reality of your circumstance."

"But I've always heard obstacles are opportunity."

"I'm not talking about obstacles, J. I'm talking about foolishness. You may be too young to remember this, but back in 1996 there was a tragic expedition to the top of Mt. Everest. If I remember right, twelve people died because the group ignored their lines of surrender. On Everest, those lines are things like not climbing without supplemental oxygen, not climbing during a storm or not climbing at night. They are guardrails to keep climbers alive. For the student-athlete, they will be different, but they *must* exist. It's part of establishing a plan."

Swap turned off the electric clippers and spun Bobby to face the mirror. "What do you think?"

"Looks great!"

Swap went about cleaning his customer and the surrounding area while Bobby continued.

"You said the rapids are an obstacle to overcome, but you're only partly right. Actually, the river is your obstacle to overcome. When the Big Shot reaches the rapids, he sees them as the obstacle and he might just try to cross. He'd be making a foolish mistake and he might die. When the PFO arrives he might consider quitting altogether. He'd be making a foolish mistake too, but he'd survive. You see, neither of them are taking the time to consider other options. My plan applies in moments of decision like this one also: Stay calm, Take inventory, Establish a plan and Put one foot in front of the other."

"So what's the right thing to do?"

"I can't tell you that."

"Why?"

"You have to book a trip to get that one." He grinned, Swap laughed, Jeff called him a tease, I wondered what I would do and Slobber scratched his left ear.

Bobby continued, "The final part of the process is the simplest yet the hardest – P. Put one foot in front of the other."

"Yep, sounds easy enough."

FREEDOM

"It is, but it requires focus and courage. Sometimes the next step is a step into the unknown, sometimes it's away from the crowd, and sometimes it will be unpopular. Will you put one foot in front of the other then? Most of the steps toward your goal are private little steps, just you and your plan. Will you take them when no one's watching?"

"I'd like to think so."

"J, the first three steps are about fifteen percent of the work. Putting one foot in front of the other is the last eighty-five percent. You just have to keep on doing it, no excuses. It has to be *your* goal, not your parents' rules or your coach's demands. Plenty of student-athletes have thrown it all away for the poison of their choice. Will you?"

"No, no I won't."

"I hope not, J. But you won't accidentally get where you want to go. Remember: Stay calm, Take inventory, Establish a plan, and Put one foot in front of the other. Do that, and you'll be just fine."

"He speaks the truth, J." Swap leaned his broom in the corner. "Bobby, thanks for coming by and talking with my grandson. I sure appreciate it."

"I'm glad it worked out." Bobby stood from the chair and shook hands with everyone in the room then spoke to me, "J, if you ever want to come to my plateau all you have to do is get there. The expedition's on me."

"Sweet." I looked at Swap, "That might have to be my new senior trip goal."

"Hold on a second now, there's one condition."

"What's that?"

SEASONS

He paused for a few seconds and took a deep breath before answering, "You can't bring Jeff." We all laughed. "See you guys later. I have to be at the church for the wedding rehearsal. Make that I *had* to be at the church. I was supposed to be there ten minutes ago."

As he walked out the door I read the words on the back of his shirt, "The adventure of a lifetime begins with the First Step."

DISCUSSION QUESTIONS

1. One of the quotes that opened the chapter said, "While we are free to choose our actions, we are not free to choose the consequences of our actions." What do you think that means?

2. Bobby said your freshman year is about survival. Do you think he was talking about life and death, or might he have been using the word in a broader sense, or maybe both? What comes to mind when you imagine "surviving" your freshman year?

3. Bobby contrasted the idea of someone arriving at camp on a gurney or on their feet. How can that metaphor apply to your freshman season (or your college years in general)?

4. First Step's survival code was: Stay calm, Take inventory, Establish a plan, and Put one foot in front of the other. If you're a college student, remember, and if you're headed to college, use your imagination, but picture that first moment on campus, independent of your family and talk about each part of the S.T.E.P. process. What are some things that could happen if someone doesn't apply these steps?

SEASONS

5. "The Quickest way to lose your freedom is to abuse your freedom." What do you think Bobby meant by that statement? Do you find yourself agreeing or disagreeing with the idea? What freedoms do college students experience that they didn't experience at home?

6. When J and Bobby were talking about the "line of surrender" the discussion featured the need to cross a river and some rapids directly in front of them. J said the rapids were the obstacle to overcome, but Bobby corrected him and said the real obstacle was the river. The point being sometimes we can hurt ourselves trying to prove something by crossing the rapids when, if we'd have followed the S.T.E.P's., we would have seen the bridge just upstream and saved a lot of heartache. If you've seen the movie *The Sandlot* this dynamic is revealed as the kids brave the "rapids" by trying to conquer the beast when all they had to do was cross "the bridge" by asking Mr. Mertle to get the ball for them. Can you think of some rapids / bridge scenarios you might face in college? Have you ever seen someone hurt themselves by foolishly trying rapids when a bridge was available? What did you learn from watching them?

– chapter two –

CONTROLLING THE MESSAGE

And I would be the first to admit that probably, in a lot of press conferences over the time that I have been in coaching, indulging my own sense of humor at press conferences has not been greatly to my benefit.
– BOBBY KNIGHT, three-time NCAA champion basketball coach

Nearly every coach I've talked with tells me that the attention you get from media and other people is the thing you miss most. I don't know if that's right.
– BEAR BRYANT, six-time NCAA champion football coach

I always mean what I say, but I don't always say what I'm thinking.
– DEAN SMITH, two-time NCAA champion basketball coach

SEASONS

IT WASN'T LONG AFTER BOBBY LEFT that Jeff finished my haircut. He brushed off my neck, removed the cloth and demanded a tip. I told him to stay married to my aunt, grabbed the sports page off an end table and sat in the neighboring chair. There were only five waiting chairs and my grandpa and I had three of them between us. Our local paper was pretty good; they covered the local college teams well and at least mentioned the bigger stories in the major sports. Except soccer. I'm actually a pretty big soccer fan and they never mention the beautiful game, not even the national team. I was reading a column, written by our local sports editor, about why Major League Baseball needed to allow some new owners into their circle. Fitting for our little town, that guy loved baseball. We couldn't spare a paragraph to talk about a World Cup, but we could send Mr. Miller, the sports editor, down to spring training every year. We don't even have a dominant following for one MLB team, yet every spring he's down in Florida writing columns about the sound of popping mitts and the smell of boiled peanuts. I was reading about the debacle with the Dodgers when the shop door opened and the second advisor of the morning walked in.

He was wearing khaki pants and a Carolina blue, linen, short-sleeved shirt that was designed to be worn untucked. Only about five feet, six inches tall and nearly the same around his waist, Tim Miller's pear-shaped body and accompanying walk were unmistakable. He heavily favored his right leg, which he claimed was injured when he ran with the bulls in Spain. Most folks believed the bull part.

MEDIA

"Morning fellas," he said as he shook my grandpa's hand and took the middle seat on the waiting row.

"Hey, Tim. Nice column today," Jeff replied.

"Thanks, Jeff. You didn't think the line about MLB divorcing themselves from owners like the celebrities in L.A. was too cliché?"

"Well, now that you ask," Jeff joked.

"I'm reading it now," I said. "I can't believe you get paid just to write your opinion about sports. You must love your job."

"I do. I set my own hours, choose my own stories and get to go to work from the comfort of my home most of the time. It doesn't get much better than that. But, in fairness to my colleagues, most guys in my field work crazy hours and are constantly under pressure. If you want to make a name for yourself in the news world, you've got to go anywhere and cover anything; it takes a lot of sacrifice. I stopped running in that rat race many years ago. I wanted a smaller town with a slower pace and found all I wanted here. Give me anonymity and freedom over fame and deadlines all day long."

"I'd die if I was anonymous. Give me the fame," I said.

"You're in high school. You probably still believe there's good music on the radio today, too," he said.

"Oh, don't tell me you're like him," I said, thumbing over at my grandpa.

"If you mean that I like real music, with real instruments, sung by real people, then I'm just like him. The synthesized rubbish you kids listen to is just that, rubbish."

"Who uses words like that? We are in America you know, in the twenty-first century," I said.

SEASONS

"But you do know we speak English, from England. Don't criticize another man's lexicon just because yours is miniscule in proportion."

"I have no idea what you just said."

"My point exactly. I'm Tim Miller, by the way, sports editor for the *Herald*." He leaned to his right and offered his hand.

"J Foxe. It's good to meet you." I set the paper down and shook his hand.

"So you want to be famous do you?" he asked.

"Sure. Other than you, who wouldn't?"

"I wouldn't," Grandpa said.

"I wouldn't either," Jeff said.

"It doesn't really count if you never could be famous Jeff," I said. "Besides, you guys are all old. I've still got life in front of me, and I want people to know who I am."

"I may be old, but I can still take you out, Junior," Grandpa said, only half joking. He didn't care for comments about his age. He actually kept himself in great shape and probably could take most guys.

"Fame is a siren, J," Mr. Miller said.

"What?" I asked.

"A siren, the seductive creatures from mythology. Haven't you read *The Odyssey*? Have teachers completely given up?" He groaned.

"Why wouldn't you just say, 'Fame is seductive'?" I asked.

"It's called a metaphor. They used to teach you about fancy things like that in high school."

MEDIA

"I know what metaphors are. I just don't understand yours most of the time. You do know you write in the sports section, right?"

"That's my chocolate cake life," he said.

"Again, what?" I asked.

"Chocolate cake, not much substance, but man it's good!"

"Now that sure wasn't cliché," Jeff said.

"This is a tough crowd you brought me into, Swap."

"Don't I know it. I live with them." Grandpa spoke with a playful grin.

"Where were we? Oh yeah, you were waxing eloquent about being famous," Mr. Miller said.

"Are you serious?" I asked.

"Sorry, I couldn't help myself. You were talking about being famous. That's kind of what I wanted to talk to you about today."

"What do you know about being famous?" I asked.

"It's not so much about being famous, but about the role the media plays in that arena. And that's something I know plenty about."

"I don't know that I follow, but okay."

"Well, answer me this. I think I remember Swap telling me you're a big fan of Christian Bale, right?"

"I like the Batman movies, yeah."

"Right, okay how do you keep up on him or those movies?"

"The Internet."

"Exactly. The Internet is simply the most modern form of mass media. Without it, and its paper predecessors, you wouldn't know anything about Christian Bale. The media covering him makes him famous."

"I see."

"The scary thing is that anyone can become famous now, for anything. It used to be that someone had to do something noteworthy for a story to be written about them. Now, with Facebook, YouTube and the blogosphere, you can become famous for ridiculous things. One needs look no further than the 'Hide yo kids, hide yo wife' guy."

"That still makes me laugh," I said.

"That's exactly why you've got to be careful, J. You run the risk of becoming famous whether you want to or not, and it may not be for football. Everybody's a reporter these days. With Facebook and smart phones, you can be an overnight success or an overnight embarrassment."

"Are you an anti-Facebook guy too?"

"Not at all. But you have to be smart with it. It's a form of media: Use it wisely. Let me bore you with the way things used to be and maybe it will help you see what I mean." He grabbed a notebook out of his pocket and began to diagram as he spoke. "It used to be that you were over here." He pointed to a stick figure on the left side of the page. "The audience was over here." He pointed to another stick figure on the right side of the page. "And guys like me were in the middle." He pointed to an appropriately shaped circle in the middle. "In order for the audience to connect with you, the media had to be the conduit; the reporter interviews and photographs the star, writes the story, and then the audience gets to read a little

MEDIA

bit about the star. In the world of sports, the media was newspaper guys, followed by radio broadcasts, then TV, then sports talk radio, then the twenty-four hour sports networks, and so on. If an athlete was smart, they would use those incredibly powerful platforms as a means to broadcast their message."

"What do you mean?"

"Consider Barry Bonds and Alex Rodriguez for a moment. They both got busted for using steroids right?"

"Right."

"But until this most recent episode, you rarely heard about Rodriguez and steroids anymore, while Bonds is still raked over the coals for it. Why do you think that is?"

"Because Bonds lied about it," I said.

"So did Rodriguez. They all did. But, to a point you're right. The two men handled their situations very differently, and that's my point. Bonds was always aloof and avoided the media, where A-Rod was a media darling. Who had more endorsement deals?"

"A-Rod, probably."

"I think so, too. Rodriguez used the media wisely. He recognized the power of their influence and used it to his advantage."

"Are you telling me to manipulate the media?" I asked.

"Yes and no," he answered. "Manipulate the system, but don't manipulate the people. The trick is to treat the guys with the mighty pens, or keyboards, with dignity. They have a job to do, and that's to write articles about you. Help them do their job and they'll help make you famous. If they ask for an interview, through the appropriate channels, show up for it and be on time. When they ask questions, answer them with a little enthusiasm, give them something to write about."

"That sounds simple enough," I said.

"It is, but it isn't. When things are going great, everybody loves the media. But as soon as they need to start asking tough questions, everybody's ready to throw them under the bus."

"Well, yeah, I get that. It seems like the media's always grilling people. Why is that?"

"Listen, in today's day and age, there are some hacks out there who sensationalize stuff and will write anything to increase blog traffic. But, even with that rogue element, pseudo-journalism, if you keep yourself out of trouble, you'll be just fine. You'll have to trust your Sports Information Department with the hacks."

"What's my Sports Information Department?"

"They serve as a buffer between you and the media. I'll call the SID and request an interview with a kid. They call the student-athlete and schedule the interview. They also produce the media guides and stuff like that."

"Cool."

"It really is. They can save you a lot of heartache, and if you're good enough, win you a Heisman. Nobody ever won a Heisman without the media telling the country about him and voting for him for that matter."

"I never thought about it like that, but I guess you're right."

"You're right I'm right," he said.

"But how does all this relate to Facebook?" I asked.

MEDIA

He scribbled in his notebook and held it up again. This time, there was a circle drawn in the middle of the page and two stick figures were standing next to each other with a little rectangle between them. Then a third figure was drawn outside the circle. "With social media and smart phones, the relationship between the star, the audience, and the media has changed. There is no longer the middle man between the star and the people; the only thing separating them is an iPhone or a computer. The media"— he pointed to the stick figure outside the circle—"spend more of their time reporting about things they're seeing and hearing from social media than they do digging for stories. It used to be hard to catch someone doing something unethical or immoral. Now, you just have to follow the right Twitter account."

"But as long as I don't get in trouble I should be fine, shouldn't I?"

"Theoretically, but it's not guaranteed. See, before social media and blogging, news guys had to fact check, verify sources and be absolutely certain what they were reporting was true. Then they had to submit stories to an editor who vetted the work and decided if it would appear in print. But now those checks have gone by the wayside. Guys like me still have to do it, but not the hacks trying to be famous bloggers. Who knows what they might write?"

"Well, then what do I do?"

"You need to think of things like Facebook and Twitter like your own personal Public Relations / Sports Information

SEASONS

Department. They are tools. Unfortunately, many athletes use them as shovels to dig their own graves."

"Now that's a metaphor I understand. Nice."

"Thanks. You have to remember that anything you tweet or post on Facebook is out there for the world to consume. If you say something foolish or post a questionable picture, you'll never live it down. And it might cost you everything."

"How could it cost me everything?"

"Do you remember, a couple years ago, the college kids that got in trouble with the agents in Florida?"

"Yeah."

"Do you remember how the NCAA found out about it?"

"Nope."

"One of the athletes posted a picture on Facebook, and the rest is history. Now understand, they got in trouble for doing the wrong things. They have no one to blame but themselves. All I'm trying to point out is that if you post it online, you better be ready to deal with the consequences."

"Well, at least I have control over what gets posted, so I should be all right, right?"

"Well, again, yes and no. Put it this way, if you do the right things and stay away from the wrong people, you should be all right. But, if you have yourself in the wrong places or you associate with the wrong people, you put yourself at the mercy of anyone with a smart phone. At that point, it is out of your control."

"You make it sound like I can never leave my house."

MEDIA

"I don't mean to, but you just better be smart when you do. You have everything to lose, so you have to be very careful to protect yourself. Not to mention, you represent the university now. Anything you do reflects on them, and if you make them look foolish they might kick you out of school."

"That sounds harsh."

"Maybe so, but they are making an investment in you and they are within *their* rights to enforce *their* rules. Your job is to represent them, yourself, your family and your little hometown well."

"I'd like to think that I will," I said.

"Just remember, the media, including social media, is a tool. You can use it to create something great, or you can use it to destroy yourself. The saying goes, 'A good craftsman never blames his tools.' Well, a good self-marketer never blames the media. Manipulate the system, treat people with dignity, don't be a fool, and the media can make you as famous as your talents will allow."

"Man, I feel like I just threw up. It was miserable at first, but now that it's done, I feel much better. I'm glad you told me all this."

"Beautiful metaphor, J. Disgusting and beautiful all at once."

"I guess it was, wasn't it?"

"Can I give you a couple tips for using Facebook and Twitter?"

"Sure, go ahead."

SEASONS

"First, set the privacy for your Facebook page to as high as you can. Make it a place where only your family and trusted friends can see what's happening. Then you need to enable the profile review option so you can control what shows up on your timeline from other people."

"But doesn't that defeat the whole purpose?"

"Hear me out. I can't stress this enough: Your personal page must remain a personal page. There is no reason guys like me or fans of your team need to have access to your private stuff. You need to have a boundary keeping personal stuff personal and public stuff public. Which brings me to my second suggestion: Start a fan page. Just start a page using your name and jersey number, or something like that, as the place where fans can 'like' the page and follow what you will *strategically* put out there for them to see. On that page you can post comments on your games, link to articles written about you, interact with fans and all that fun stuff. But all those people don't get to comment on the pictures of your family at Christmas or whatever."

"That actually sounds pretty cool. My own fan page, nice."

"And if you want to use your name, you can try this: Change your personal page, or maybe start a new one using your real name or your middle name. Then make your fan page your everyday name. Those that need to find you will, and the public will find your fan page."

"That's probably what I'll do actually."

"Either way's fine. Now about Twitter. You have to think of Twitter as a professional tool, almost like an ever-changing

MEDIA

resume. I *strongly* encourage you to resist using it as a place to share personal stuff or make loose comments about the world. Think of it as an extension of your fan page. In fact, I would link the two accounts. Use it as a marketing and promotional tool, otherwise, you stand a great chance of being hurt by it for being foolish."

"You make it sound so serious."

"That's because it is. Too many people are careless with it and they hurt themselves or their loved ones. I had an electrician working on my house one day and he told me how they assume every wire is hot, even if the power's off. He was saying it's just not worth getting electrocuted to save a couple seconds. I think that's a great way to think about social media. Just like electricity, it can do good things for you, but if you are careless you'll get shocked."

"I hadn't realized how crazy that whole world is. I mean I've seen crazy stuff out there, but I never really thought about it affecting me."

"If you're thinking about it now, then this has been time well spent."

"I'm thinking about it now for sure."

"Good. Swap, Jeff, J, I need to scoot. I was supposed to be at the stadium for a press conference about five minutes ago. Thanks for letting me talk with you," Mr. Miller said.

"Thank you for coming by," my grandpa said.

"It was surprisingly informative," Jeff kidded.

"I really appreciate it. I learned a lot. Thanks," I said.

"Well, all right then. I'll see you guys another time. Cheerio!"

SEASONS

Tim Miller left the shop and headed into town. He lived downtown and could walk to almost anywhere he had to go, including the ball park. I picked the paper back up and finished Tim's column. He really was a good writer.

1. J said early on how he wanted to be famous and many of us hold that secret desire. Mr. Miller then shared how people can become "famous" for less than noble reasons. If you do have dreams of fame talk about specifically what you'd like to be famous for. What are some examples of ways you would *not* want to become famous?

2. Fame is an interesting idea. Sometimes, when we say we want to be famous we are really saying we want to be very wealthy. So let's take money out of the equation. Researchers say one of a person's greatest fears is to be anonymous, to be unknown. Nobody wants to be forgotten and ignored, not even the introverts. Becoming famous seems like the exact opposite of that fear and a potential remedy for that issue. Yet somehow we continue to read stories of famous people who are still lonely and in successive, unhealthy relationships. How do you think it's possible to be famous but still lonely? And if fame isn't the true antidote for loneliness, what do you think is?

SEASONS

3. Why do you think it would be a good idea to treat the members of the working press with dignity and respect? If you are famous, and many student athletes are local celebrities, how could the way you treat the people in the local media help or hurt you?

4. What did you think about the advice Mr. Miller gave about using Facebook and Twitter? Have you ever posted any words or images on a social media platform you regret? It may seem unnecessary at first, but what are some benefits to keeping your personal page personal and creating a fan page for the public to use?

5. The Golden Rule says, "So in everything, do to others what you would have them do to you ..." Using the context of social media and iPhones, restate that idea in a practical, literal sense. For example, "Only post pictures of friends I wouldn't want posted of myself." Come up with as many example as you can.

6. Mr. Miller used electricity as a metaphor for the media, saying it is a wonderful, powerful thing, but that it can also shock you if you aren't careful. What are some things you can do to make sure you are more careful when you use social media and interact with the press? What are some things you can do to protect yourself from other people using social media in careless ways?

–chapter three–

SCHOLARSHIPS AND SPENDING

Money... is like a beautifully trained thoroughbred horse – very powerful and always in action, but unless this horse is trained when very young, it will be an out-of-control and dangerous animal when it grows to maturity.
– DAVE RAMSEY, author and financial advisor

If you can, you will quickly find that the greatest rate of return you will earn is on your own personal spending. Being a smart shopper is the first step to getting rich.
– MARK CUBAN, owner of the Dallas Mavericks

I guarantee you, I spent a million dollars on jewelry.
– ANDRE RISON, five-time NFL Pro Bowl wide receiver

SEASONS

I WAS STILL LOOKING THROUGH THE SPORTS SECTION when another man walked in Swap's Shop. He was just short of six feet tall and wore a black suit, minus the jacket. Sandy blonde hair covered most of his head, but gray was peeking out around his ears. He looked like a politician, but in spite of that appreared to be a down-to-earth guy.

"Hey Swap!" My grandpa got out of his chair as the man walked up to him and gave him a hug.

"It's great to see you, Jim. I'm glad you could make it."

"I never could resist your negotiations," the man said. "Besides, my hair's gotten a bit out of control, so I could use your services."

"That's an understatement."

"Easy, Swap. It's not that bad."

"Well, it will be respectable when I'm finished. Sit down here." Grandpa spun the chair to face his client. "Jim, this is my grandson, Justin Samuel Foxe the third; we all call him J."

I felt good whenever my grandpa used my whole name. It made me feel like he was proud of me, like he wanted people to know I was his.

"Nice to meet you, J. I'm Jim Moore. Your crusty old grandpa cut my hair back when I played third base at Spalding. Now, I work for Northeast Financial, up in Greensboro. I help people develop personal financial plans and Swap asked me to talk to you about your money."

"I hope you have some sort of plan for $300 'cause that's all I have," I said.

MONEY

"We'll get to the plan in a minute. First, I want to offer a little perspective. I understand you're going to college in the fall, full scholarship, right?" Mr. Moore had taken the seat next to me and my grandpa was slowly prepping him for a haircut. Jeff and Grandpa had turned our chairs to face each other while we talked.

"Yes sir. They want me to play linebacker," I said.

"That's good, J. Congratulations. I'll tell you what, the next few years of your life are going to be pretty incredible. Obviously, it's been a few years since my days."

Jeff interrupted, "You mean a few decades."

"Who's counting? Anyway, it's been quite a while since my days as a college athlete, but I remember them well. There wasn't much scholarship money back then, so I paid my own way even though I was a four-year starter and was all-conference my last three years."

"And you played third?" I could tell he wanted to talk about it, so I humored him.

"The best third base around. I didn't hit for power, but I could go get that baseball. I was quick. Yeah, I don't think I hit five home runs over my whole career, but I don't think I made five errors either. The guys all called me Brooks because I played like Brooks Robinson."

My grandpa stopped cutting his hair, stared down at him, and said, "They just *called* you Brooks?"

"Okay, okay. I told everyone to call me Brooks. Geeze, you Foxes can sure ruin memories. But I did play just like Robinson. I even wore his number five."

SEASONS

"I don't know that we're ruining your memories as much as we're keeping you from 'misremembering' them, Mr. Clemens," Jeff said.

"Oh, so leaving out where I got my nickname is the same as being questioned for steroid use? I don't suppose you've told J all your little secrets? I'll never be bringing my sons to get their hair cut in this shop. Who knows what they would think of me after you two CSIs finished your interrogation."

"Okay, *Brooks*, I'll stay out of it. I think you were just comparing yourself to the greatest third baseman of all time; please continue." Grandpa laughed and shook his head as Jeff bowed out of the conversation.

"Did you play in the majors?" I asked.

"I wish I could say yes, but I never got the chance. We didn't even have a minor league team within a hundred miles of us. I doubt the big league clubs even knew I existed. My dad was a pretty no-nonsense guy, so he wanted me in the workforce as soon as I graduated anyway."

"So, what do you do?"

Mr. Moore's face became a little more serious as he answered, "Like I told you, I'm a financial advisor. I help people with investing, retirement plans, college funds, what have you. I used to work for one of the big companies but I've been on my own for about ten years now."

"J, I asked Jim, I mean Brooks, to come talk with you about what you are really getting from State and to give you some advice about having a plan with your money," Grandpa said.

MONEY

"That's right. So, do you have any idea how much your scholarship is worth, J?" Mr. Moore asked.

"To be honest, I've never thought about it."

"That's all right, most kids haven't, most kids who are getting scholarships at least. If you were going to be paying your own way next fall you would know how much it costs, I'll guarantee you that. You're staying in-state, which is great. But did you know the national average for a year of school at a major public university is around $22,000?"

"So what's that, about $5,500 a year?" I asked.

"No, son, $22,000 per year. That's including room and board, fees, meals, books, everything. A college education costs over $80,000 these days. That's not counting going to the movies or putting gas in your car. Not to mention, as good as you are, you'll still probably redshirt."

"The coaches already said they want me to take a redshirt, said I need to gain about twenty pounds."

"So, there's another $22,000. Now you're looking at $110,000 for your education, plus expenses and you're not paying a cent." Mr. Moore was very matter of fact.

"Yeah, but I heard it doesn't cost the school anything. I heard it's just an extra kid in the classroom and no one actually pays for the scholarship. That's why I think college athletes should get paid."

Mr. Moore adjusted in his chair. "You need to stop listening to sports radio and get in the real world. You're partially correct though; your scholarship won't cost the school anything.

SEASONS

But that's because the booster club and the athletic department pay the school for your education."

"Really?"

"Really. Universities have professors to pay and campuses to maintain; they aren't giving classroom seats away. When I write the booster club a check, it goes towards the athletic department's expenses. The bulk of the money goes toward scholarships. At your school, it's the same way, just on a larger scale."

"Okay, so it still doesn't cost the school anything, and they get millions from TV. They're cleaning up. The athletes should get a cut," I said.

"Listen, when you run *your* business you can decide how to split your profits. Until that time, you need to worry about what *you* can control. Besides, the last time I saw the data, fewer than twenty universities showed a profit in their athletic departments. Big time college football brings in a lot of money, but big time college football costs a lot of money too. All those millions you speak of go right back into running the program. Personally, I think paying athletes more than they already receive, would absolutely ruin college sports and ruin the college athletes."

I interrupted, "What do you mean, 'More than they already receive?' Do they get paid already?"

"Not paid, per se. You'll never see most of that $110,000, but you will get some spending money. For instance, the book store will have your name in its system and you'll just have to show your student ID to pick up your books. The

MONEY

other kids will be standing in line to spend $400 on theirs for the semester. You will also receive a little money on top of having your expenses paid. It's there to cover things like doing your laundry, gas and a little fun. We aren't talking about a big amount, but it's enough to get by."

"That's just it," I said. "Why should we just get by? We're making the school millions."

Grandpa shot back, "You're not making that school anything. You're being given an education and you might never contribute on the field. They're speculating against your potential. Even still, you're being given an opportunity most kids never get."

"Besides," Jeff jumped in, "'Just getting by' is part of the college experience. Everybody will be searching their couch cushions for money to go to the movies; it's part of it. Why should it be any different for you?"

"I don't think it should be different for me, but other kids aren't required to go to practice every day."

"You're right, J. But those other kids also don't get their school paid for or get the privilege of playing big time college sports. And plenty of them will be going to jobs while you go to practice," Jeff said.

"And playing the game isn't free, J." Mr. Moore nudged my grandpa out of the way to look me directly in the eyes. "I did a little research from some friends in booster clubs at some of the big schools to get an idea of how much they spend on players in a season."

"You mean like paying for classes and stuff?"

SEASONS

"No, that's all in the scholarship. I'm talking about uniforms, meals and trips. They said it costs around $1,300 a year just for uniforms and equipment for each player."

"I didn't know that."

"Neither did I, which is why I asked. They said they pay about $800 per player for each road trip. That's over $4,000 for a five-trip season. Shoot, even the home games cost about $250 per player. Taking it all in, there's another $7,000 in extras you'll receive every year."

"Wow. I'd never thought about it. I guess that's pretty cool though. So, Grandpa, is that what you meant about getting an opportunity most kids never get?" I asked.

"No." He stopped working on Mr. Moore's hair and looked at me through the mirror. "I mean going to college. Just getting a college education, regardless of who pays, places you in the upper half of society. We're talking about paying you for going to school when most kids are looking for an entry level, $10 an hour job to start their career."

"He's right J. Consider this. Research shows, as a college graduate, you will earn at least $20,000 a year more than someone who didn't go to college. That's about $1,700 a month you'll have to go toward a nicer house, savings, family vacations, whatever. Your scholarship is buying you an education that will earn you an extra $600,000 over a thirty-year career. That's not bad," Mr. Moore said.

"When you put it that way—"

"I'm not finished. Think about the other college students. Most of them are taking out student loans to pay for school.

MONEY

That means that when they begin their careers, they'll be swimming in debt. You have an upper hand on the high school grads and you have an advantage over the college grads that paid their own way. J, if you can wrap your mind around this opportunity, you can really improve your future. Did you know that your scholarship will pay for graduate school?"

"No, but I don't even know what I'm majoring in."

"Did you take any AP courses or any dual enrollment classes?" he asked.

"Actually, yes, I've already got eighteen hours of college credit," I said.

"You're in great shape then. If you push yourself a little, you can graduate in three years and get two years of grad school paid for. Not only would you be getting roughly another $20,000 a year of higher education on the house, you stand to make much more than a student who only has their Bachelor's degree. Motivated kids are doing it more and more. You'd be wise to do it yourself."

"That's pretty cool. I didn't know I could do that," I said.

"Have you ever heard of compounding interest?" he asked with a grin.

"Nope."

Jeff stopped cutting and focused on Mr. Moore. Henry was on his back with his legs moving like Usain Bolt. He must have been dreaming about chasing Pop-Tarts. Grandpa kept working on Mr. Moore's hair but was looking at me to make sure I was paying attention.

SEASONS

"Check this out. Your peers, who paid their way through school, are going to be paying about $400 a month to their debt for the next thirty years, and that's on the low side. That's $4,800 a year. Now, you won't have those payments, so let's pretend you're wise and invested that $4,800 a year over that same thirty year period. When you've finished, you'll have invested $144,000, but you'll have accrued just under $870,000!"

"Wait, how?" I asked.

Mr. Moore grinned, "It's called *The Rule of 72*. Assuming your investments earn a ten percent return, your money will double basically every seven years. Over the thirty year period, your money will have doubled four times, and you end up with close to a million dollars. If you're smart, you'll invest more than $4,800 as you earn more income and you'll have even more."

"That's tight," I said. "I had no idea."

"That's exactly why I asked old Brooksie to come speak to you, J," my grandpa said.

"J, you've been given a fantastic financial opportunity and the best piece of advice I can give you is to take a couple finance courses while you're in school."

"Why is that? What if I don't want to work at a bank or do what you do?"

"Because you don't know how money works. Very few people really do and it's a shame. Most people only see money in terms of right now – I got paid $500 today so I have $500 cash for the weekend. Very few people are thinking about their futures until it's way too late. Because people don't know how it works and don't have the future in mind, they just spend."

"Right, but you have to spend it. You have to eat, have a place to live and stuff."

"You're right. But where and how you live isn't fixed. When, where, and what you eat isn't fixed. What you drive. Shoot, *if* you drive. None of that is fixed. Every one of those things represents choices, and what a person decides reveals what they understand about money."

"How so?"

"Let's pretend you got a job tomorrow making $24,000 a year, so $2,000 a month."

"Okay."

"You need to get back and forth from work so you decide to buy a car. And since you're young and looking for a girl you decide to get a nice, new car with a big $500 a month car payment. Now you have less than $1,500 a month to pay taxes, rent and insurance; to buy groceries, electricity and water; to go to movies, take a vacation or date this girl you want to impress. The math just won't work."

"But what if I get a better paying job?"

"That statement tells me all I need to know. Trust me, J, you will thank me later if you get educated on how money works."

"What did I say that was so wrong?"

"Instead of thinking in terms of managing what you have and living within your means, you just wanted to have more to buy more. That kind of thinking is what gets people in trouble and keeps credit card companies in business. Let me give you an example. You were arguing earlier about how student-athletes should get paid. The problem is that there is no end to that game. When it comes to money, we are like water. We'll fill whatever financial container we're placed in, and in most cases, overflow it. In other words, we'll run out of money before we run out of month. Without a plan, your spending will just rise as your income rises. You said you have $300 to you name, right? And are you surviving?"

"Yeah, of course. But I don't have any expenses," I said.

Mr. Moore looked at me through the reflection while my grandpa ran the clippers on the back of his neck. "And you won't have any in college. Somehow you are surviving with $300 to your name, yet you feel you are in a position to demand the school pay you. Let's say they did. Let's say they gave you an extra $500 per month."

"That would be sweet!"

"Sure, but you know what would happen? You would fill that container and before too long be complaining that $500 a month is insufficient. The issue isn't income. The issue is money management. Instead of thinking about putting money away so they have a little saved up when they graduate, most kids are just thinking about where they can go out to eat Friday night. Unfortunately, most student-athletes and, to be fair, students in general, don't fully appreciate what they're receiving and, in turn, don't manage themselves well financially. They just spend. Shoot, most people don't manage their finances well, and it's because they just don't know how

MONEY

it all works. This is why you should take a finance class. I promise you will be so glad you did."

"It would teach me about that *Rule of 72* and stuff like that?" I asked.

"I guess it depends on the professor, but you'll learn so much more. Outside your major work, it will be the most valuable class you take, and it might be the most valuable, period."

"Well, I'll keep it in mind, but I just hate math and it sounds like a semester of numbers and formulas."

"I hear that from people all the time. Don't think of it in terms of a subject, think about it in terms of your future and providing for yourself and your family. If I told you I would give you $870,000 to take the class, would you?"

"Twice."

"Alright then. So, outside a finance class, the best thing you could do is start to live on a budget."

"A budget?"

"Yeah. Think of it like a game plan. Each dollar is a player and your budget tells them what to do. Most people have no plan, so they just live week to week and never get anywhere. Well, I take that back. They get somewhere — stuck in a big hole of debt."

"What do I do?"

"It's really not that complicated. First, set a few goals so you have something to focus on. Then figure out how much you have coming in, what your fixed expenses are—"

"Fixed expenses?" I asked.

"Yeah, like rent and your water bill."

SEASONS

"Oh."

"And you will have almost no fixed expenses because the school will cover all that. Once you know what they are, though, you put together a little game plan for reaching your goals. You'll set a little aside according to your plan and be able to spend the rest without worry."

"Sounds simple enough."

"It is, especially in college, but as you get older the budget gets more complicated because you add people and fixed expenses. You'll be doing yourself a big favor to develop the discipline now, while it's easiest."

"Fair enough, but can you give me some idea of a financial goal?"

"Sure. Think short term goals, like getting yourself a used car for school. Then some long term goals, like a senior year spring break trip to Australia. And then really think about your future, like retirement and stuff like that. Really, the goal is whatever will help you focus and develop the skills necessary to manage your money, so pick something you would really love and think of it as an investment in your future. A particularly wonderful investment."

"Australia would be awesome."

"Then go for it. I don't know how much a flight to Australia costs, but you can look it up, and once you have an idea you can plan accordingly. Figure out how many months till your trip, divide the cost by that number, and you'll have what you need to save every month. While your buddies are spending another week in Panama City using a credit card,

MONEY

you'll be Down Under on a trip that you've already paid for. That's a g'day in my book."

"That would be a sweet trip," I said.

"Having the goal is the key, and then just spend less than you earn and you'll be fine. Take the finance course and pay attention. Appreciate everything you have. I guess I'm saying just be grateful," Mr. Moore said.

"You know gratitude isn't an emotion, J. You might not feel great about everything, but you can still choose to be grateful." Grandpa's words rang true. I've never heard him complain about anything.

Mr. Moore jumped back in, "You've got a good head on your shoulders, J, and you've got some men here who care about you. Listen to them. Let this information sink in, think about it. If you play your cards right, you can maximize your experience as a student-athlete and set yourself up for a great future."

Grandpa spun his friend's chair to face the mirror. "How's it look?" he asked, referring to the hair cut.

"Looks great, Swap. As always."

As my grandpa brushed off the cloth, Mr. Moore had a little more to say. "J, as a rule, if you'll concern yourself with managing the money you have, as opposed to hoping someone will give you more, you'll be surprised with how strong of a foundation you can build. If you're wise with a little, odds are you'll have plenty more to work with as you mature. Count your blessings, manage your budget, put a little away, and you'll be just fine."

SEASONS

"Thanks Mr. Moore," I said.

He shook Jeff's hand, hugged my grandpa, and left Swap's Shop. I noticed that he drove off in a sweet little ride.

DISCUSSION QUESTIONS

1. At the start of the chapter was a quote from former NFL Pro Bowl wide receiver Andre Rison. He said it in the ESPN 30 for 30 documentary called *Broke*. Just think about his words and talk about what they reveal about his situation, "I guarantee you I spent a million dollars on jewelry." Do you think he was being boastful or speaking with regret when he said that? Why do you think that?

2. When you think about how someone donated money from their personal savings to pay for your scholarship what does that reality make you feel? Imagine if you gave someone a $100,000 gift. How would you hope they would treat it?

3. What did you think about the way Mr. Moore explained how valuable a scholarship is contrasted with having to use debt to pay for school?

4. Mr. Moore challenged J when he said, "Instead of thinking in terms of managing what you have and living within your means, you just wanted to have more to buy more." Talk about what you think that means. Why do you think it is so enticing for people to spend everything they get as opposed to saving some of it? Why do you

think people spend more money than they earn to establish their lifestyle?

5. It was suggested that you take a finance class in college, but many people hate math and want nothing to do with a course involving that many numbers. Acknowledging it might be a tough course, what do you see as the potential benefits to taking one of those classes?

6. Share some ideas for short term financial goals for a college student. Share some fun ideas for some long term goals, like a senior trip. Are any of these ideas compelling enough that you would take the time to put together a budget and discipline yourself to honor it? Why or why not?

–chapter four–

EXPECT IT AND ATTACK IT

Show me someone who has done something worthwhile, and I'll show you someone who has overcome adversity.
– LOU HOLTZ, NCAA champion football coach

Adversity is the state in which man most easily becomes acquainted with himself, being especially free of admirers then.
– JOHN WOODEN,
Ten-time NCAA champion basketball coach

Adversity causes some men to break; others to break records.
– WILLIAM A. WARD, author

SEASONS

Mr. Moore wasn't gone two minutes before another car pulled up. It was a black SUV with deeply tinted windows. Even though I'd never met the man, I knew who it was as soon as I saw his car. Jackson James grew up across town from my old house. He'd dominated high school ball and gone on to the University as a pitcher. He led them to a couple College World Series appearances and was drafted in the first round by the St. Louis Cardinals. After only a year and a half in the minors, they called him up and he ended up playing thirteen years in the bigs. In his sixth year, he was an all-star and ended his career with almost one hundred seventy wins. If he hadn't hurt his back he might still be playing, although he says he was set to retire, back injury or not. He retired two years ago and moved back to town to open a baseball academy. He and his business partners broke ground at the new property in June and are supposed to open in the spring of next year. A lot of families are hoping Jackson's baseball school will be the ticket for their sons to follow in his footsteps.

He didn't dress like he drove. His car was classic big city, big leaguer, but his clothes made him look like every other guy in town. He had on a pair of jeans right out of a Brett Favre commercial, a Jimmie Johnson T-shirt and a store-bought Cardinals hat. He was every bit of the six and a half feet his baseball card said he was.

"How are you, Jack? I appreciate you making time for us," Grandpa said as the man entered the store.

ADVERSITY

"It's a slow day over at the academy property, just grading the ground for one of the infields. Anyway, I wanted to meet the legendary J Foxe I'd read so much about. Is this the man?"

"Yes sir, I'm J. It's an honor to meet you. I've read a lot about you, too." As soon as I said it, I remembered what Tim Miller said about the media making people famous.

He laughed as he shook my hand and then flopped into the vacant barber chair next to me. "I can't believe you still have that picture, Swap," he said, pointing to a picture of himself as a little league player, standing with my grandfather.

"Are you kidding, Jack, that's better than any old baseball card. Nobody in St. Louis has one of those I'll bet."

"You're right about that, and it's a good thing. I can't believe my mom let me keep my hair that long. If you hadn't convinced me to cut it, I'd have never gotten married," he said to my grandpa.

"No truer words have ever been spoken son," Grandpa said. "So, you need a cut today?"

"No thanks, Swap, I don't think I have time. The wife wants me to drop by the house to meet with the countertop salesman. She's ready to get out of the townhome and into our new place, so these appointments are non-negotiable."

"Hey, you do what you've got to do," Jeff said. "When my wife was pregnant, she had the same attitude while we converted the guest bedroom into a nursery. I never knew there were so many shades of yellow, and I never thought I'd be arguing between Daffodil and Meadow Wildflower."

SEASONS

"I don't think I'd tell anyone else that story, Jeff," I said, as the guys laughed.

He looked down at me. "And what would you know about it Mr. High School? One day you'll be sitting in a store, debating which dessert fork matches your china pattern. Then you won't be so quick to judge."

"I'll let my wife take care of it. I won't be wasting my time on frilly stuff like that," I said.

All three men closed their eyes and shook their heads, almost in unison. Grandpa laughed under his breath and broke the silence. "You've got a lot to learn boy, a lot to learn."

"I guess that's my cue," Jackson said. "Your grandpa asked me to drop by and talk with you about my career. But I don't really know where to begin, so why don't you ask me some questions and we'll see where that takes us."

"I'd love to."

"But first, I understand Thomas Cothran's coming by later. He's the guy to ask about your beliefs on china patterns. He and I went to high school and college together, and we were the best man in each other's weddings. He's the best family man I know, so save those questions for him. Let's you and I stick to sports."

"Fine with me," I said as Grandpa took a seat in one of the waiting chairs. "How was it? I mean, tell me about playing pro ball."

"I'm not gonna lie. It was everything I hoped it would be and more. There is nothing like standing on the mound in a big game, surrounded by forty thousand of your fans, staring

ADVERSITY

down a guy like Chipper Jones. I got to throw from the same mound that Bob Gibson and Dizzy Dean used. I played on the same field as Stan Musial and Ozzie Smith. It was a dream. As you can imagine, the money was good and the fame certainly had its perks, but there were negatives too. We were on the road three months every year for games, not counting spring training. Even the best hotels lose their glamour after a while. But I've got no complaints. Playing a professional sport has to be the best job in the world."

"That's tight! I can't wait to get there. But, I won't have to travel anywhere near as much. I'll only have eight away games a year," I said.

"Slow down there, Ditka. Listen, for every story like mine, you've got a thousand stories like your grandfathers. If what they say is true, Swap could've had a long major league career, but one injury can change the way the story ends. Injuries aside, the minor leagues are full of high school All-Americans and college phenoms."

"Yeah, I've heard that stuff before, but I'm a football player; it's different."

"Maybe you're right, but you never know. I was in Georgia for a charity golf tournament and the Bulldogs' head coach, Mark Richt, was there giving the keynote speech. He might have been a Pro-Bowl quarterback, but he never got the chance to play. His story is one of being in the shadows of greatness. Three different times he was the backup to an eventual Hall of Fame quarterback, so he never saw the field as a pro. The sport may be different, but the principle's the same

— the odds are overwhelmingly against you becoming a professional athlete, and even worse that you'll make a career out of it."

"So, what, I'm supposed to just give up my dream then? All anybody ever wants to tell me is how impossible it is to make it to the NFL, but I didn't expect to hear it from you, too," I said.

"J, I'm not trying to crush your dreams. Shoot man, I was a dreamer, too, and I got to live it. When I talk to high school kids, one of the things I tell them is, 'Sure, only one percent of high school athletes play in the pros, but, one hundred percent of pro athletes played in high school.' The point is, you have to know the odds and develop an overcomer's attitude. Sir Edmund Hillary didn't mistake Mt. Everest for a small hill before he reached the summit. He knew he was setting out on an impossible journey that might cost him his life and he prepared like it. You have to develop the same resolve."

"The last guy who was here said something about a trip to Everest, too. I'm beginning to wonder if I need to plan a trip."

"You can have that trip, J. I'll keep these two feet planted squarely at sea level."

"Not a big fan of heights?"

"It's not so much the heights that bother me; it's the idea of falling from them that's scary. I used to make everyone close to me close their window shades when we flew and I still freaked out. Most flights, with the exception of when I was pitching the next day, the team doctors had to sedate

ADVERSITY

me. It was pretty bad. That's actually how I got the name 'Light's Out.'"

"That's how you got that name? I thought it was because you struck out so many people."

"The media gives you nicknames for reasons like that. Your teammates give them to you for reasons like mine. The guys are good about keeping you humble."

"It makes me wonder about some of the nicknames floating around out there," Jeff said.

"And your suspicions are probably true. But what were we talking about before I started complaining about flying?"

"Something about Mt. Everest and resolve," I said.

"Oh yeah. Here's truth, J, adversity is going to come. You have to expect it and be ready to attack it when it rears its ugly mug. You might show up to training camp and find out the guys at your position are better than you. What will you do then? Will you quit? Will you abandon the dream?"

"No way! I'll just beat them out."

"What happens when you tear your ACL the summer before your sophomore season? Playing time was right in front of you, but now you will miss the whole year. Are you gonna sulk? You gonna pack it in?" Jackson asked.

"Well, I guess I'll get surgery and go through rehab. Right?"

"Exactly, but you have to understand, rehab is a lonely place. Just you and a doctor, working as hard as you ever have before, with very little progress and nobody telling you you're a superstar. Plenty of good athletes have fallen prey to a difficult rehab. Quitters don't go through rehab."

SEASONS

"Jack, I can assure you that J is no quitter," my grandfather said.

Feeling more confident, I said, "He's right, I'm not a quitter."

"I believe you. But my point still stands. Adversity will come and you have to be ready to attack it. Injuries and competition are the least of your worries though. The really tough stuff comes within the team. What are you going to do if the guys in the weight room are having a lazy day? Are you gonna be lazy, too? What happens when you guys lose a few games and guys start complaining? Are you gonna complain, too? What if you guys win every game you play? Complacency has ruined many teams and even more players. How will you respond when the adversity of success hits you?"

"You make everything sound like a problem," I said.

"You haven't heard me say the word problem one time. I'm talking about adversity, J. Have you ever seen Mt. Everest? There's not a horizontal piece of rock on the whole mountain. Playing in the NFL is like reaching the top of Everest – you will climb every day of your career, nothing's horizontal."

"Yeah, but—"

"There's no 'but,' J. As soon as you think you've reached a plateau, the other guy is getting a higher foothold and you're falling behind. I don't care how talented you are or what school you're going to, you're a dime a dozen. Everybody's got talent in the league. Everybody was an All-American. Everybody went to a big school. Guys in the league are climbers; they don't settle till their careers are over. Then they

ADVERSITY

go climb something else. If you want to play pro football, you have to prepare for an impossible journey that might cost you everything. It's Everest."

"Listen, J," Grandpa said, "all he's saying is that you have a huge dream. And it requires a huge person to accomplish a huge dream. You have to have a tireless work ethic, an unshakeable determination and an uncommonly positive attitude. You have the talent to make a run at it, but if your determination and attitude don't keep pace with your talent, you'll never reach the top."

"Exactly," Jackson said.

"J, don't let this discourage you. It's a small boulder at the foothill of your mountain; it's a little adversity. You've got to hear it, process it and then attack. That's what we're trying to get you to see," Jeff added.

"Then what am I doing wasting my time with you guys? I need to go work out or something," I teased.

"Whoa there, tiger," Jackson said. "You need to prepare your heart and mind, just as much as you prepare your body. I can't tell you how helpful a conversation like this would have been for me as a high school kid. I whined and moaned through things that greater men cruised through. I only spent a year and a half in the minors, which is unheard of. If I'd have had to spend three to five years in those farm towns, I might've hung it up. I wasn't ready for adversity."

"But you made it so far. You were an all-star," I argued.

"Let me tell you something, J, and this stays here in Swap's Shop. Can I trust you?"

SEASONS

"Sure, you can trust me," I replied.

"I wasn't ready to retire before I hurt my back. I wasn't in my prime, but I was still one of the top pitchers in the league, and if I'd have kept on my pace I could've won three hundred games. I doubt if I'd have been a Hall of Famer, but I was gonna give it a run. When I hurt my back and the doctors told me I was looking at missing an entire season to rehab, I lost my nerve. I figured I'd never make three hundred if I missed a whole season. I didn't want to spend a year doing yoga and watching my teammates play on TV. So, I quit. Saying I retired sounds better, but the truth is, I quit."

"Gosh, Jackson, don't you think you're being a bit hard on yourself?" I asked.

"Absolutely not!" His eyes began to water. "I quit, J. My career had been a breeze and at the first sign of adversity, I shrunk back. The summit was within reach and I quit. It was the poorest decision I've ever made. I regret it all the time." The room was silent for a few moments while we gave Jackson James, town hero and self-proclaimed quitter, time to gather himself. He continued. "You just have to be ready to fight for what you want; that's all I want you to hear. You can't let a critic, a competitor or a challenge keep you from climbing. But, and listen closely to what I'm about to say, if you don't make it to the league, you cannot quit life."

"What do you mean?" I asked.

"I see it all the time, man. Guys will completely sell out to make it to the top. Never-surrender kind of guys. But they didn't have the talent or for some other reason they weren't

ADVERSITY

able to reach their goals. Sadly, these guys will go in the tank because they feel like failures. Their personal lives crumble, their marriages fall apart. It's tragic. Don't be that guy, J. Not being a quitter applies to more than sports, it's a whole life attitude." Jackson said.

"He's right again, J, but I've got someone else dropping in today who will talk to you about some of those issues," Grandpa said.

"Sorry to get so heavy. I didn't expect it to go there," Jackson said.

"It's cool," I replied. "I'm glad you did. They don't put that stuff in the newspaper articles."

"Do you have any other questions, maybe something a little lighter?" he asked.

"Actually, yeah. What pitch did you throw when Chipper hit that walk-off against you?"

"Oh, so now you've got jokes? I hung a curve, if you must know," he said.

"That was the only day I remember cheering against you. Sorry, but I love my Braves," I said. "It's his fault." I pointed at Swap.

"That's fine. But refresh my memory, how many World Series titles do your precious Braves have?"

"Two, I think?"

"Three, actually," he corrected. "Look at the bright side, they only need to win two more in order to have half as many as my Cardinals. So Chipper got lucky and the Braves beat me, big deal. We still have the most championships in the National League."

"Well, we'll see what happens this year," I said.

"Hey, the Braves and Cards are playing in a couple weekends, why don't you come by the house and we'll watch together. I'll need somebody to tease," Jackson said.

"Really? I can come to your house?" I asked.

"Of course, you can help my wife select curtain material."

With that, Jackson James popped out of his seat, said his goodbyes and left the shop. As he stepped into the mid-morning sun, he pulled his red cap down over his eyes. It isn't every day you get to hang out with a big league pitcher, but I had a feeling we'd be hanging out some more over the summer.

DISCUSSION QUESTIONS

1. What are your thoughts on this statement from William A. ward, "Adversity causes some men to break; and others to break records?"

2. Jackson said adversity was inevitable and that, "You have to expect it and be ready to attack it when it rears its ugly mug." What are your thoughts on what he said?

3. One of the great things about sports is the relationship between teammates, but a long rehab from an injury can be incredibly lonely. What are some things you can do to prepare yourself for that possibility? What are some things you and your teammates can do to help someone else go through a long rehab?

4. Talk about the adversity of criticism and share some examples of when you've experienced it in your life. Do the same thing with the adversity of praise. Knowing that both criticism and praise can be adversity, what are some things you can do to prepare yourself for them?

SEASONS

5. Many of us dream of reaching the highest level in our respective sport, be it the Olympic Games or the NBA. Jackson warned against "quitting life" if you aren't able to reach that goal. What do you think "quitting life" means? How can you balance the idea of striving toward the highest goal while also preparing yourself for the possibility of not reaching it?

– chapter five –

RELATIONSHIPS

THE GOOD ONES ARE GOOD, THE BAD ONES ARE BAD

I won't miss coaching. What you miss is that camaraderie with those boys and the other coaches. You miss that.
– BOBBY BOWDEN, two-time NCAA champion football coach

*You have to work hard at staying in contact with your friends so that the relationships will continue and live on...
Friendships, along with love, make life worth living.*
– MIKE KRZYZEWSKI,
four-time NCAA champion basketball coach

SEASONS

The sun was arcing closer and closer to its apex, and my hunger was doing the same. I ran down to the drugstore and picked up a Snickers to hold me over; lunch might not even be on the schedule for today. I had about two-thirds finished and was laughing at the word "Chewjitsu," written on the back of the wrapper, as I walked back into Swap's Shop. There was a man sitting in each of the barber chairs. Jeff was cutting the hair of a tall, thin man, while it appeared the man in my grandpa's chair was there to talk to me.

"J, I want you to meet Reggie Cutchings," Grandpa said.

Reggie wore a warm smile and offered his hand. His gentle manner bore a sharp contrast to his intimidating stature. At six foot six and at least two hundred fifty pounds, Reggie looked like he could still strap a helmet on and wreak some havoc in an NFL backfield.

"Good to meet you, J. I've heard a lot about you," he said.

"It's nice to meet you, Mr. Cutchings."

"You can call me Reggie."

"OK. Then it's nice to meet you, Reggie," I said.

He grinned and even though I knew he was humoring my subtle attempt at humor, his face was sincere. He seemed trustworthy.

"Do you mind me asking what you were laughing at as you walked in?" he asked.

"No, it was nothing. I just get a kick out of the ridiculous words on Snickers wrappers. This one says, 'Chewjitsu.'"

RELATIONSHIPS

His eyes lit up as he spoke. "I love those. The best one I saw was on a billboard in New York. It said, 'You're being dunked on by Patrick Chewing.'" His smile faded at my response.

"Is that supposed to sound like someone?" I asked.

"*Is that supposed to sound like someone?* Are you serious? Swap, is he serious?"

"He's a football guy, Reggie, what can I say?" Grandpa said.

"J, Patrick *Ewing* was one of the best centers in the NBA. When I was playing football at Rutgers, the campus was only about forty miles from Madison Square Garden. That's where the Knicks play basketball, in case you didn't know."

"I know about the Garden," I said, trying to improve my first impression.

Laughing with my grandfather, he continued. "My freshman year was 1989, so from '89 through the end of the '93 season, my friends and I were Knicks fans. A couple times a year we would go to Manhattan and watch a game. Ewing was a beast. He was an all-star every year I saw him play, and that was at the height of their rivalry with Michael Jordan's Bulls. You've heard of him, right?"

"Of course, he's the underwear model who's in all of Kevin Bacon's commercials. C'mon, I'm not sports illiterate," I answered.

"How can you know Jordan and not know Ewing? It's like thinking there's only one political party in America or that planes only have one wing. Those guys battled for championships in college and in the NBA. Then they played on the "Dream Team" together."

SEASONS

"I guess I might have heard of him, but he's obviously not as good as Jordan, otherwise I'd know who he was," I said.

"He wasn't even as good as Olajuwon," Jeff's customer chirped.

"I don't know about Olajuwon, but Jordan certainly had his number. The Bulls knocked my Knicks out of the playoffs three years in a row. We lost to the eventual champs every year I was at Rutgers: The Pistons that first year and then the Bulls on their first three-peat. As good as Ewing was, he didn't have a good enough supporting cast to get by Jordan and Pippen."

"Actually, J," my grandfather said, "that's a good segue. Even if a person is great, if his supporting cast isn't, he'll have a hard time reaching his goals."

"Your grandfather asked me to come by and share my experience with you. Do you mind if I talk with you for a while?" Reggie asked.

"Sure. You're the first person to ask my permission. The other guys just jumped right in."

"Your grandpa and I go way back, known him since I was about your age. He helped me through some rough patches in my life, but I've grown up a little since those days and now I'm a pastor over in Beckett. I spend countless hours working with people who are struggling, just like your grandfather did for me when I was younger."

"That's cool. I actually know a few guys over in Beckett. We met last summer at a football camp. One of them is going to State with me. He's the best wide receiver in the state."

RELATIONSHIPS

"You must be talking about Derrick."

"Yeah! Derrick Freeman, from Lincoln High."

"I've known that boy since he was in diapers. His family was a part of the church when I first started."

"He seems like a good guy."

"He is. He's still a foolish teenager, but he's a good young man. His daddy is a fantastic man. Other than Swap, Derrick's father is the most important man in my life. He took me under his wing when I first started and has shared his life with me ever since. I consider him one of my closest friends. If Derrick turns out to be half the man his father is, he'll be one of the great ones."

"We have been talking about rooming together at school so that's good to know."

"He would be a good roommate; you guys would be good for each other actually."

"I'll make sure to tell him you think I'd be a good influence on him."

Reggie smiled. "Go right ahead. Just remember, I'll ultimately have the last word and I'm sure Swap wouldn't mind sharing some good stories so I can give Derrick a good idea of the guy he's gonna be living with."

"I've got a few in mind already." My grandfather was never one to pass up on a chance to mess with me. "I think he'd love to hear about the time you tried to tackle one of the cows out at the Clark's farm."

"I know I would," Jeff said. "How have I never heard about this?"

"You tried to tackle a cow?" Reggie asked.

"We don't have time for this. You were getting ready to talk to me about something and I'm sure it's more important than one of Swap's ridiculous stories."

"Fair enough," Reggie said, grinning.

"You know I'm gonna have your dad fill me in, so that's fine," Jeff said.

"I'm sorry," Jeff's customer said, "I don't know you, but Steve Clark owns the land next to me so I'll just get the story from him. I sure hope his cow was able to survive the trauma."

They all enjoyed their jokes for a few seconds before Reggie finally picked up the conversation, "I'm here to talk about one of life's great paradoxes."

"What's a paradox?"

"It's what a sailor says when he comes up on two places to park his boat, 'Hey, captain, it's a pair of docks,'" Jeff laughed. The other men stared at him. I shook my head.

"I'm referring to an idea that might appear to contradict itself or might be both positive and negative."

"Like saying Jeff's funny?"

"Or J's good looking?" Jeff grinned, proud of his little joke.

He laughed. "No. Those are both oxymorons, and while true, they're not really paradoxes. Imagine being so hungry you were almost starving and the only food I had to offer was a handful of ghost peppers. That situation would be a paradox. You know you have to eat, but eating the food you have in front of you might be worse than starving."

RELATIONSHIPS

"I saw a guy eat a ghost pepper once and I literally thought he was going to die. I think I'd prefer starving to death than what I saw happen to him."

"The paradox I want to talk to you about is relationships."

"Now you've lost me again, but I assume you'll tell me how a relationship is a paradox."

"When trouble comes, good relationships can help you weather the storm, though sometimes it's relationships that cause the storm to begin with. We were made for relationships and need them for a fulfilled life, but they often cause us great pain. Broken relationships are one of the reason's I'm in business, so to speak."

"That's why Swap asked you to talk with me then, I guess."

"That's partly true, but he also asked me to come because he knows my story and he wanted you to know it too. So, I want to start with a little rule to live by; it sums up this whole little talk we're about to have. You ready?" he asked.

"Sure, go ahead."

"Good relationships are really good. Bad relationships are really bad. Make sure you have good relationships," he said.

"Sounds simple enough," I said.

"As a principle, it is. In practice, it can be challenging. Emotions get involved, situations get complicated, and you end up seeing as gray things that are actually black and white."

"What do you mean?" I asked.

"Let me tell you what happened to me. Well, I shouldn't say 'happened' because it makes me sound like a victim. The

SEASONS

truth is, I made some poor choices and had to face the consequences. But, for lack of a better term, here's what happened," he said.

"Start with how you ended up at Rutgers, Reggie," Grandpa said.

"I've always wondered that. I thought you were a lock for State," Jeff said.

"I don't talk about it too much, Jeff. But it's certainly pertinent in this case. J, I was being recruited by all the big schools. I'd been all-state for three consecutive years as a defensive end and won All-America honors as a senior. One paper said I was the best prospect in the state for the class of '89."

"Then I'm with Jeff. What possessed you to choose Rutgers?" I asked.

"Well, when it came down to it, they were the only ones who'd have me," he said. "During my senior year I got into some trouble."

"What happened?" I asked.

"More like *who* happened. Again, I am the only one responsible for my choices, but when I started running with a couple shady characters I started making some pretty stupid decisions. It was relatively harmless at first. We'd cut a class and go off campus to grab lunch or sneak into the movies, silly stuff. We actually got caught a couple times, but people would let it slide because I was sort of like a celebrity."

"You should have been hanging with Reggie, Jeff. Maybe he could have helped you with your dreams of fame," I joked.

RELATIONSHIPS

Jeff finished cutting the man's hair and was accepting his payment, so all he could do was grin and bear it.

"Fame's not all it's cracked up to be. It's actually one of the reasons relationships can become puzzling. Unfortunately, since I didn't get in trouble for my little crimes I ended up pushing my limits further and further. To make a long story short, the three of us stole a car over our Christmas break and ended up wrecking it."

"Whoa, what did they do to you?"

"I got off pretty easy on this one too, at least from a criminal perspective. They gave us two hundred hours of community service and we had to pay the man to have his car fixed."

"Was the guy mad?" I asked.

"Why don't you ask him yourself? It was Swap's car."

"Wait. You stole my grandpa's car? Why? He's never had a nice car."

"Watch it there, sport. That pick up out there is a classic," Grandpa said. "Anyway, Reggie spent the bulk of those two hundred hours working for me and we became pretty close. It's funny how things work sometimes."

"So, things turned out all right here, but as soon as the big schools caught wind of my arrest, the scholarship offers were rescinded. Rutgers was the only school willing to take a chance on me, and that's only because your grandfather vouched for me," Reggie said.

"That was nice, Grandpa, but why'd they listen to you?" I asked.

SEASONS

"They didn't. I had an old friend who ran a business in New Brunswick, so I called him and asked for a favor. I told him the whole story and he went to his friends at the school and explained the situation to them. Really, it was my friend vouching for you that did it, Reggie."

"See, J, good relationships can be really good. Bad relationships can be really bad. You've got to be so careful when you choose your friends, and you *do* choose your friends. I can't tell you how many young people I've counseled who blame their neighborhoods or teammates for their foolish choices, but I tell them exactly what I'm going to tell you: You can't be passive in your relationships. The good ones require effort, and that effort is one of the best investments you'll ever make. The Bible says, "He who walks with the wise grows wise, but a companion of fools suffers harm." I was running with fools when I stole Swap's car, but I was able to spend about two hundred hours walking with the wise. And, as a result, I made some better choices when I got to New Jersey."

"I bet you were pretty motivated when you got to two-a-days," I said.

"Boy was I. I felt like I'd been given a second chance and I was going to make the best of it. However, it seemed like no matter how hard I worked I couldn't get the coaches to trust me. They knew my past and they were on me like syrup on pancakes. If I was a minute late to a meeting, they acted like I'd broken the law. If I missed a class, they pounced. But you know what? It's exactly what I needed in those first couple years."

RELATIONSHIPS

"Were you still getting in trouble?" I asked.

"No, it wasn't that so much. I just needed the discipline and perspective. Because of what happened in high school, I wasn't looking to make friends for a while. The coaches were the closest things I had to friends, and it was a good thing. There were some older guys on the team who'd become bitter for some reason. They complained about everything and did their best to infect the younger guys with their same rotten attitude. Bad relationships right there, J."

"So, what happened?"

"Well, I didn't mean to, but I became a leader with the younger guys. The only way I can explain it is I did what I was supposed to do and had enthusiasm doing it. I was just trying to do my job well, and the guys respected that. The bitter older guys didn't, but it didn't take much for them to be marginalized," he said.

"Were you getting playing time?" I asked.

"I got in for a few mop up snaps my first year. Then, I was splitting time with one of the seniors my sophomore season. He was actually a good guy and a solid player. My junior year I became the starter and stayed the starter until I graduated."

"Nice! You were pretty good then I guess."

"I wasn't bad, but the whole celebrity thing showed up again. We weren't nearly as good as the Rutgers teams from a few years ago, and football wasn't anywhere close to that popular, but the players still had a bit of star power. I received most of the attention because I was one of the best on the team and I was getting some NFL attention."

"I bet you had plenty of friends."

"Well, that's just it. Friends were still hard to come by. I had plenty of people who wanted to use me. We called them 'remorons'," Reggie said.

"Remorons?"

"One of my friends on the defensive line was from the coast and began calling the hangers-on remoras, after the fish that attaches itself to big sharks. It wasn't long until remoras became remorons, and the name stuck," he said.

I laughed, but then asked, "So, how did you figure out who your friends were?"

"For the most part, it was guys on the team. I was with them all the time anyway, and they understood what being a student-athlete was all about. There were some pretty good guys in my class. Most of your friends will probably be players too, but you still cannot be passive. You must separate the wise from the fools and avoid the fools. There's a time to lead them away from their foolish ways, but not until you've got some wise friends in your life."

"I'm glad you said that because I was going to say while you were walking with the wise, as you called it, my grandpa was the companion of a fool, and it's a good thing he was. I think it's important to try and be friends with everybody."

Grandpa jumped in. "You're right, to a point, J. I had many years and a whole heckuva lot of experience under my hat before I met Reggie. And I wasn't looking for a friend. I saw a kid who needed a little guidance and I tried to offer some.

RELATIONSHIPS

When you are looking for friendship, it's tough to lead anyone."

"He's a wise man, J. This is the emotional aspect of it; desire can cloud your judgment. Here's what I mean. Imagine a middle school kid who desperately desires to be accepted. Because his desire is so strong, he's likely to compromise to get what he wants. People do it all the time and call it sacrifice. Most bad things are just good things at inappropriate times, with inappropriate people or with inappropriate motives."

"How's that?" I asked.

"Well, if I sacrifice time from my wife so that I can go to a strip club, that sacrifice is a bad thing. But, if I sacrifice a little comfort to help someone in need, the sacrifice is good. See what I mean?" he asked.

"Yeah, I get that. But are you telling me that strip clubs are sometimes good?" I joked.

"No, but it still applies. Men are supposed to desire women; it's a good thing. A strip club is taking that desire and placing it in the wrong location, at the wrong time and on the wrong person. That same desire focused in a healthy way on your wife is a good thing." he answered.

"Easy for you to say, you're married. I've got plenty of desire, but I'm not allowed to act on it, ever," I complained.

"Believe me, I know how you feel. But let me encourage you: save *all* that desire for your wife and you'll be happier in your marriage. Think of it like crossing a street in downtown New York. You have the freedom to cross at any moment, and you might make it across unscathed. But the odds are that you'll end up getting hurt and hurting others along the way. If you wait for the right time and the right place, like at the crosswalk with the walk sign lit up, you'll cross safely and avoid the heartache. I ended up with heartache."

"Really, can you tell me what happened?"

"I'll tell you, but this is a sensitive area, so I'm trusting you guys here." I could see in his eyes that he wasn't just being dramatic.

"I think you're safe to tell them, Reggie," Grandpa said.

"In my junior season I started getting some attention from the ladies on campus. One particular girl captured my attention and I was hooked. We started spending a lot of time together and our relationship continued to escalate, as is normally the case. Well, I figured that crossing the street was inevitable, so I decided to cross on my own terms. All seemed well at first. I figured I was one of the ones who crossed unscathed, until she showed up at my apartment late one night. I could tell she'd been crying, and she didn't speak. She just handed me a note and literally ran away sobbing. I figured she was breaking up with me."

He paused for a minute, and then asked, "Swap, do you have anything to drink?"

"Sure do. Jeff, will you toss him one of the waters from the fridge please?"

Jeff flipped him a water. Reggie opened the bottle, took a long drink, and then continued. "She didn't just break up with me, she broke me. The first line read, 'I was pregnant.' That sentence said enough and I crumbled. She continued to say

RELATIONSHIPS

that it was her body and she didn't want to worry me with the responsibility, so she aborted the baby. So much for crossing unscathed. That was the most frightening and drastic swing of emotions I've ever experienced. The indescribable joy of finding out I was a father, smothered with the searing pain of finding out my child was dead was crushing. It was like taking a bite of a big piece of chocolate only to find a rancid fish inside – sweet for a moment but retching in the end."

The shop was silent while Reggie shared his story. He'd told the story before, but I could tell that time hadn't lessened his pain.

"I wonder about that child every day. I don't know if it was a boy or girl, but I didn't like referring to him as 'it,' so I decided on a boy. Did he look like me? Would he have loved sports? I know it sounds crazy, but even though I never met him, I miss him terribly."

"It's not crazy, Reggie. It's absolutely natural," Grandpa said, being a pastor to the pastor.

"His mom dropped out of Rutgers and I never saw her again. I don't blame her at all for what she did. She was scared, and I'd given her no reason to trust me. I would have married her, but like I said, she had no reason to trust me. I hate that I put her in that position and would have loved to help her through it, but that's not how the story went. I pray for her all the time; it's really all I can do. The reason I'm telling you all this is just to give you another perspective. You probably won't go through what I went through, I realize that. But the message being broadcast in culture today is that promiscuity is harmless and it's really no big deal. That's a lie, J. Even if no one ends up pregnant or with an STD, there are scars when you cross that street prematurely. Trust me."

He took another long drink from his bottle of water and I said, "I do trust you, Reggie."

"I'm glad, because I'm telling the truth."

"So what did you do?"

"I called my mom. She always seemed to know what I needed, and she did then too. She actually came up to New York for a couple days to hang out. My friends complained at first," his serious expression began to turn and his eyes lit up as he spoke, "but after she made dinner that first night they were happy to have her. I'm tellin' you, that woman could flat out cook."

"That's cool, but I tend to agree with your friends. I don't want my parents snooping around when I'm at college."

"I understand that," Reggie said, "but, J, the way you treat your family says a lot about who you are as a man."

"I've heard people tell me for years my friends are what reveals who I am because I picked my friends where my family was given to me."

"There's truth in that, but let me put it to you this way. Do you know how to play poker?"

"I know Texas Hold 'em."

"That'll work. Taking cheating out of the equation, what would it tell you about a person if you found out he stacked the deck when you played him?"

"That he's a cheater."

RELATIONSHIPS

"I said, taking cheating out of it."

"Then he's a punk."

"Right, right. But I mean, what would it tell you about his knowledge of the game?"

"Well, I guess it depends."

Reggie looked surprised by my answer and said, "Depends on what?"

"It depends on his cards. If he's stacked the deck but gave himself a bad hand it would say he doesn't know the game at all, just how to cheat. But if he gave himself pocket kings I would know he understands the game. But I'd still call him a cheater."

"That's a great answer, J. I want you to think of your friends kind of like that. There are a whole lot of people you'll be able to choose from, some are threes and some are aces. You'd be a fool, and show your ignorance of life, if you loaded your hand with threes. You see what I'm saying?"

"Yeah, I like that. I just need to keep good people in my life to give myself the best chance of winning, so to speak."

"Exactly. Good relationships can be really good. Bad relationships can be really bad."

"But what does this have to do with family?"

"This is what separates the great from the good. Your example was accurate; you don't get to choose your family so think of them as the hand you're dealt, no fooling with the deck. You got dealt a good hand. Me, I got an ace and six, off suit – my dad was a questionable guy."

"Well, you turned out all right."

"Sure, I was dealt another ace on the 'river.' Swap saved my game."

"So, you're saying I just have to be patient with my family and see what happens?"

"No, not at all. I'm saying you've got to become an excellent player. Anybody can win a hand with a full house, but only the great players can win with bad cards. The masters know their hand is only part of the game. They read other players and they know situations. Beginners only focus on the cards in their hand. That's why they have terrible poker faces."

"I've got no poker face whatsoever. I'd get killed by a real player."

"You've got to see beyond the cards in your hand and play the game well, regardless. The same is true with family. You have a great family, but if you get cocky and take them for granted you'll lose your advantage. You need to appreciate them, learn from them and keep them close. But if you had a bad deal I'd tell you the same thing. Bad cards don't make the player, great players make the cards. If your dad had been a bad dude, like my dad, it wouldn't give you the excuse to give up. You'd still have to play the game well. But you don't discard him either. He's your father, good man or bad man, and you need to appreciate him, learn from him and keep him close."

"Wouldn't that be walking with a fool?"

"Well, kind of. This is the tricky part. You've always got to remember the rules of the game are more important than your cards. In fact, it's the rules that determine what your cards are worth. That being said, some players can keep a

RELATIONSHIPS

bad pair of pocket cards close and still win hands by playing the game well. J, nobody gets to choose their family, but when it comes to friends we get to see the deck. If a man was dealt a bad hand, he'd be a fool to select cards just like the ones in his hand. I guess I'm just saying choose good friends, but never forget your family. You'll need all your cards in the end, even if a couple aren't so good."

"I think I understand."

"Just remember what I told you at the beginning; good relationships can be really good, but bad relationships can be really bad. Make sure you have good relationships."

"I'll certainly try," I said.

"You really can't afford to try, J. You need to make it happen," Grandpa said.

"I will, Grandpa."

"Reggie, thanks for being so open with us. I really appreciate your candor," Grandpa said as he helped Reggie out of the chair.

They hugged and Reggie said, "I just hope it helps. This is a really cool thing you are doing for J."

He reached over to shake my hand. "Just be smart, son. A companion of fools suffers harm. I don't care what religion you profess, that's true. If you've got any questions or if I can be of any help, your grandfather knows how to find me; call me anytime. But Swap probably has better advice anyway, so you can just ask him. I had to steal his car to get it."

We laughed and Reggie headed out into the bright afternoon.

DISCUSSION QUESTIONS

1. A big theme in this chapter is how we desperately need relationships but how relationships can cause us intense pain. Talk about some of the important relationships in your life. Then talk about why you think those relationships have the potential to produce such heartache.

2. Reggie repeatedly said, "Good relationships are really good, bad relationships are really bad." What do you think that means. Talk about examples you've seen of really good or really bad relationships.

3. The old proverb about walking with the wise or being a companion of fools was brought up. Why do you think people can be so influenced by the people they're "walking with?"

4. When J challenged the idea of avoiding fools by pointing out how Swap had walked with a fool when he was helping Reggie, Swap responded by saying, "I wasn't looking for a friend." Why do you think desiring to have someone as your friend would affect your ability to influence them? How do you think that desire could affect their influence over you?

RELATIONSHIPS

5. What did you think about the story Reggie shared about the girl from college?

6. Reggie talked about family and friends using a card game as a metaphor. What did you think about that idea? Which cards do you think are the most important, the ones you were dealt or the ones you place in your hand? Why?

−chapter six−

IDENTITY

WHO YOU ARE, WHO YOU AREN'T

*You've got to be careful. You can't become what you do.
What I do is not who I am. If I become
what I do and I become just a football coach,
then you're asking for disaster.*
– MARK RICHT, two-time SEC Coach of the Year

*If you're just saying, 'Hey, I'm doing this,
I'm working to make money. I'm working to increase my status.'
If that's all there is, I think you'll find out that's meaningless.*
– TONY DUNGY, two-time Super Bowl winning coach

SEASONS

Swap's Shop was a nice little place. People loved going and spending time there, even if they weren't getting a haircut. But for all its charm, it seemed to stay hot in the summer. Every time the front door opened, the cool inside air rushed for the outside like elementary kids being released for recess. A ceiling fan or two would have been nice, but Swap was concerned they would make it hard to cut hair and make loose hair circulate through the shop. He was probably right. Jeff walked over and turned the AC down a few degrees. I thought about running up to the gas station on the corner to get a drink, but the thought of being outside kept me in my seat. I picked up a magazine and fanned my face instead. Slobber was panting like he'd just finished a chubby dog triathlon. I wasn't sure he was going to make it through the afternoon. "Jeff, you may want to get Slobber some water while you're up. I think he's lost his motivation to walk." Jeff grabbed the dog's bowl from the bathroom, filled it with cold water from the tap and placed it in front of the sweating bulldog. Slobber dragged himself up to the bowl and flopped his head into the water, flipping the bowl on its side and soaking himself and the floor.

Jeff groaned, "Slobber!" Swap and I laughed while Jeff went to get the mop. Swap didn't seem phased by the temperature and as Jeff was cleaning up the mess. He said, "Neither of you would make it on one of Bobby's expeditions if you can't handle the heat. This is nothing compared to what you'd face down there."

IDENTITY

"At least there would be water close by and I'd swim with a crocodile to get out of this heat," I said.

My magazine fan was still working nicely when a woman walked into the shop. She was thin, in her thirties I guessed, with brown, lightly highlighted hair stylized out of a trendy magazine which framed her face. A white, sleeveless button-down shirt hung untucked over a pair of khaki shorts and her black flip-flops smacked the floor as she stepped inside. She pulled her sunglasses from her eyes and slid them to the top of her head, pulling her hair out of her face in the process. I noticed she had a wedding ring on the same hand, but it made complete sense seeing how her left arm was missing, apparently amputated above the shoulder.

"It's so hot, Mr. Clark's cows are giving evaporated milk," she said.

Swap quickly followed suit, "It's so hot, I saw a bird using a potholder to pull a worm from the ground."

My mind began racing to come up with something to say. Jeff must have had one ready, "It's so hot, I saw a dog chasing a cat and they were both walking."

They were all smiling. I was thinking harder than I had in any of my exams. The woman kept the game alive, "It's so hot, the Statue of Liberty has pit stains."

Swap again, "It's so hot, I saw a chicken lay a hard boiled egg."

"It's so hot," Jeff said, "there's hot water coming out of both taps."

SEASONS

They laughed some more, then Swap said, "It's so good to see you, Laura." He walked over and gave her a hug.

"It's good to see you, too, Swap. You wouldn't recognize Gage. He's up to here on me." She held her hand next to her right hip. I don't know why exactly, but she didn't look like the kind of woman who would name her son Gage. Maybe it's because I have a friend named Gage and his mom hunts more than most of the guys I know, drives a Ford F-150, and wears camo pajamas.

"J, Jeff, this is Laura Thompson. I went to school with her daddy—"

"I've got one!" I said. "It's so hot, I saw Optimus Prime transform into an air conditioner."

"That's good," Laura said, smiling. "My husband will like that one. He loves Transformers. I don't get it personally, but he watched the cartoons as a kid and would probably have us sleeping under a Transformers bedspread if I'd let him."

Swap helped her into his barber chair. "J, Laura was a world class tennis player a few years back. She was a junior national champion and qualified for the U.S. Open as a fourteen year old. Her last two years in college, she was an All-American and began tearing up the pro circuit after she graduated. But she's not playing tennis on the level anymore, and that's part of the reason I've asked her to come talk with you today."

"How are you, J?" Her smile made me think she was really curious to know how I was doing and not just saying hello.

"I'm good. It's been a full day already but a good one."

IDENTITY

"I can imagine it's been a lot to swallow. Swap told me what he was doing with you and I've been thinking about you and praying for you ever since."

"I hope you don't take this wrong, because I really do appreciate it, but why would you be praying for me?"

She laughed softly, but not at me. I was worried she might be offended or think it was a stupid question, but it's like she thought my question was sweet. It was the same way my mom looked at Tyler when he asked her questions like "Why is the sky blue?" or "Where does thunder live?"

"I tried to picture what it would be like to have a bunch of strangers visit me and give me advice I hadn't asked for." Her smile grew larger and she blushed just a little. "It may sound silly, but I pictured Ebenezer Scrooge when the Ghost of Christmas Past came to visit. He was so resistant, so defensive, so fearful, and I didn't want you to feel that way. So, I've been praying that you wouldn't be intimidated or fearful today, and that you might find a joy similar to the one old Mr. Scrooge experienced when his visits were finished."

"Your prayers have been answered then." Swap paused and I could feel a corny punch line coming. "He's not said 'Bah Humbug' one time." She seemed to like Swap's – well, I guess some would call it – humor.

"I just wish you would have prayed for a little Christmas weather. I could go for a snowball fight about now," Jeff said.

"Me too," Laura said.

"It's too bad I have to be the grown up around here, but thank you, Mrs. Thompson. It really hasn't been like you feared. I don't know if it's 'cause you prayed or not, but I've enjoyed each of the people who've come by today and I'm looking forward to the ones to come. It's been pretty cool, actually."

"Well, I'm glad. I'm not really sure what I'm supposed to say to you today, but I figured I'd just start by telling you about my arm and see where the conversation leads."

"That's okay by me."

"Like your grandfather already said, my life was tennis growing up. I don't remember when I first held a racket, but I was very young. Both of my parents played recreationally and they would take me with them to the courts. While I was there, I started playing around. They never pushed tennis on me, but they didn't have to. I've loved the game for as long as I can remember being aware of it. It wasn't long before our roles reversed and my parents were going to the courts to watch *me* play. They taught me the basics and helped me develop my game, but there was a talent there that none of us could take credit for, and I won every little kid tournament I entered. We spent almost all of our free time at the courts. I'd play against mom or dad sometimes and every once in a while I'd play against both of them at the same time. It was always a lot of fun, but it started to become a big part of my identity. My friends knew me as Laura, the tennis player. My parents and I seemed to only talk about tennis. I didn't have any other hobbies and the people I looked up to were great tennis players. I did well in school, but I could tell you far more about the history of Wimbledon than I could the Civil

IDENTITY

War. After I won the Junior National Championship, tennis had officially supplanted Laura as my defining idea. It had previously been when people would think of me, they would think of tennis. But after that win, when people thought of tennis, they thought of me, and I started feeling pressure for the first time. No one intentionally made me feel that way, but there's only so many times you can hear, 'Can't wait to see you on TV one day!' or 'Be sure to remember us when you make it big!' before you feel like you'll be letting people down if you don't make it."

"You know," I said, "I've actually felt that way, too. I haven't had the success you had, but people still talk about seeing me play on Saturdays or how they hope I'll be drafted by their favorite NFL team. I've always thought it was kinda fun, but there is an expectation there too. I hadn't really thought too much about it because I feel the same things, but the thought of not making it is where the pressure builds."

"It was the same for me," she said. "When I was playing and having success, I loved that stuff. But if I ever struggled, those affirmations of future success turned into accusations of unmet expectations and they could smother me sometimes."

"So what did you do about it?"

"Nothing. What *could* I do? I wasn't going to tell people to stop supporting me, so I just embraced it and worked that much harder to make sure I didn't let anyone down. And I was successful. I got a full scholarship to play at Stanford and was All-American my junior and senior seasons. Both years I lost in the finals and finished second in the nation and that was a big disappointment, but it just pushed me to work harder still."

"Who beat you? Is she still playing?"

"That's actually a funny story. You've never heard of her because she had no interest in playing professionally; she entered medical school as soon as she graduated. But because we spent so much time at the same places with tournaments and training, she got to know my older brother and they ended up getting married. Her name's Lacy McDonald. She's a pediatrician in California and the mother of my two nephews."

"Small world, I guess."

"Especially in the world of tennis. Anyway, I was moving up the ATP rankings and gaining international respect, but in February of 2001, I was in a car accident and everything changed. My husband, Brent, and I were in the Florida Keys for our honeymoon. I was driving us to dinner and felt as relaxed as I had in years. We were slowly cruising along the road. I was taking in the view of the ocean and had my arm sticking out the window, waving it in the breeze. All of the sudden, a big delivery truck swerved into our lane and before I had a chance to think, our car was folded around a palm tree. The impact caused some bumps and bruises, but no serious damage to us because, like I said, we weren't going very fast at all."

"Then what happened to your arm?"

"Well, right as we left the asphalt, another palm tree scraped the side of our car and when it did, we lost the

IDENTITY

driver's side mirror and my left arm. It was crazy, because I didn't feel anything. I don't know if it was shock or what, but I didn't process what had happened until we'd stopped and Brent asked me if I was okay. I started to speak, but when I looked down and saw the blood but couldn't see my arm, I passed out. When I finally came to, I was laying in a Miami hospital with one fewer appendage."

"Did they try to fix it? I mean, couldn't they have sewn it back on or something?"

"They tried. There was a volunteer fireman who saw the whole accident and was at my side almost as soon as our car stopped moving. I had no idea, of course, but Brent told me when I woke up. He had already called 9-1-1 from his truck and when he got to us, he calmed Brent down and had him retrieve my arm. While Brent was doing that, he dressed my wound and worked to stop the bleeding. When Brent came back with my arm, the fireman prepped it for the hospital, and by the time the ambulance arrived, both me and my arm were ready to be transferred. Despite all that, they still couldn't reattach my arm, but they said the fireman might have saved my life by reducing my blood loss to a minimum. The next morning, while I was still knocked out from surgery, he came by and brought Brent a change of clothes and took all our car rental information and handled all that stuff in the lobby so Brent could stay with me. He was incredible. I met him the next afternoon and he visited every day until we were discharged. His name was Gage Brantley, and we named our first son after him."

SEASONS

"That guy's a hero. I wouldn't have had a clue what to do if I had been the one on the scene. I would have probably passed out. So, what did you do? After you got home I mean."

"That's when it got hard, J. It was a shock to wake up and realize I'd lost my arm, but learning how to live with one arm and dealing with the reality that my tennis career was over was almost too much. I was resolved and tenacious, but you just can't be prepared for something like that. Initially, it was just the physical challenges, but the more I had time to think, the more I sunk into a depressed state because of tennis."

"You just missed playing?"

"If that were all it was, I think I would have been okay. There are ways to play the game with one arm. My sadness was tied to all the expectations I would never live up to and the question of who in the world I was without tennis to define me. My sister-in-law had a plan and knew who she was, but I had no idea. Tennis was all I knew. Tennis was my identity and now I was nothing. At least that's how I felt at the time."

"What do you mean when you say tennis was your identity?"

"I mean it was all-consuming. My closet was full of tennis clothing. There were tennis magazines lying around my house. Most of my conversations centered on my career or the game in general. I soaked up all the attention my success got me and loved being kind of a big shot. I lived and breathed tennis. Does that make sense?"

"Absolutely. It's my life now. My mom's always trying to get me to talk about something else or do something away from the game. She says she doesn't want my life to orbit football."

IDENTITY

"See for me it got even worse than that. I thought my life orbited tennis, but eventually I realized the yucky truth that my life revolved around me, and tennis was the way I made it happen. I was one big ego. It was key that I realized it when I did. Tennis was gone, but I was still there, and since I was the center of my own universe I could easily have replaced tennis with something else. In fact, I'd already started to."

"With what? Could you work?"

"Sure, but I had been a professional tennis player. My work was on the court and in the gym. Coaches gave me undivided attention. My trainers gave me undivided attention. There isn't another job that could replace all that ego building. I didn't want a job; I wanted another reason for people to make me the center of attention again. I found what I was looking for with my lost arm, and simply replaced the adoration of praise with the adoration of sympathy."

"What does that mean?"

"Have you ever seen someone get hurt or something and milked it for all it's worth?"

"My little brother Tyler does it all the time. I also knew a guy who fell down in gym class while we were playing basketball. He whined on the floor for a while, but he got up and was fine. Sure enough, the next day he showed up to school on crutches and kept them for weeks. It was so lame."

"That's what I did, but I was really hurt so people were willing to help. And I manipulated that situation for all I could. I was more than willing to tell the accident story or lament about my tennis career. I especially loved when people would talk about how great I had been and how successful I would have been. I realized that because I never really failed, I could live up to their expectations in a fantasy world of what might have been. I was still a hero and people loved being able to help me. They would buy me meals, do my grocery shopping, wash my car, anything really. Brent got it the worst though. I treated him like a peasant and arrogantly asked him to do everything for me. Not because I couldn't, but because I didn't want to, and I liked being served."

It was hard to picture the woman talking to me as the woman she was describing. She was so humble and kind, but the woman she was talking about was a monster. "It's hard to believe you were like that."

"That's nice of you to say, but I was. I let my identity get wrapped up in what I did so it was easy for me to become a narcissist. It was an ugly time for me. During that time, I got pregnant and we had Gage. Having him brought my self-centeredness into full view for me. He didn't care about my tennis career and he didn't care about my arm. If he was hungry, he cried. If he was tired, he cried. I found myself competing for attention with a human less than a year old and it hit me that I was acting just like him. I was acting like a self-consumed child and when I asked Brent about it he was courageous and loving enough to tell me the truth and confirm my fears. I was a *me monster*; Brent actually used the term 'Self-a-saurus.'"

"He'd been thinking about that," Jeff said.

"Yeah, he was," I said.

IDENTITY

"Oh, there's no doubt," she said. "I was just amazed he hadn't called me out sooner. Thankfully, Gage's infantile selfishness revealed my symptoms and Brent's precise diagnosis helped me realize the truth, and I started to change."

"What, you just stopped complaining and stopped asking for help?" I asked.

"No. See, it was deeper than that. Being without tennis or my arm wasn't the problem, *I* was the problem. I was tempted to become hyper-independent, but I realized I would just be doing the same thing. First with tennis, then with helplessness, and finally with proud self-reliance; it was all narcissism. The truth is, I needed help and I needed people who cared about me and for me. No, I had to discover my true identity and let that fuel the change."

"I'm guessing you figured that out. What was it?"

"I'm not sure I know exactly."

That wasn't the answer I was hoping for. "What changed?"

"I began to discover things that didn't define me, and that's what began making the difference."

"What didn't define you?"

"The first thing I latched onto was being a mother. I figured that was who I was. But the more I identified with that idea, the more attached I became to it. I could tell because of how I responded to criticism and praise, or lack of praise. If Brent would suggest a new way of dealing with Gage, I would get deeply offended as if he had called me a name or something. And if things were fine and Brent wouldn't go out of his way to tell me how good I was doing, I'd be deeply offended for the same reason. I quickly found out I couldn't find my identity in my role as a mother. Then I did the same with my role as a wife, and again with my side job as a book keeper for a few non-profits. Each time I tried to make my identity something I did, I discovered it wasn't true."

"How does knowing that make you better?"

"I probably wouldn't use the word 'better.'"

"What would you call it?"

"I prefer healthier."

"Okay. How did learning that make you healthier?"

"When I stopped claiming my identity in my tasks or roles, I was able to receive criticism objectively and receive praise without becoming arrogant. I no longer got offended if something wasn't working with Gage. I stopped feeling heavy burdens to please people or be perfect."

"Alright, but where are you now? Or maybe, who are you now?"

"Like I said, I'm still figuring that out. I know I'm not 'Laura, the tennis player' or 'Laura, with one arm,' even though people might describe me that way. I'm not Brent's wife or Gage's mom, even though both of those things are true about me. Just like you play football and are Swap's grandson. They're true, but they aren't all you are. My current challenge is to discover who I am and why."

"Well, you have me thinking but frustrated, too. I can understand not letting football define me because one day my career will be over and I'll still have to live on. That makes sense. And I can follow that with other things, too, like a job

IDENTITY

or career. I just wish you could give me something more positive about where to look."

"I know what you're feeling, but I found some hope in a quote from Thomas Edison."

"He's the light bulb guy, J," Jeff said.

"Thanks. You sure about that?" I shook my head.

Mrs. Thompson continued, "Edison was asked about failing as he was trying to invent the light bulb and he said, 'I have not failed seven hundred times. I have not failed once. I have succeeded in proving that those seven hundred ways will not work. When I have eliminated the ways that will not work, I will find the way that will work.' I take that same approach to figuring out this identity question. Each time I eliminate a false identity, I am one step closer to finding the true one."

"So there's no easy answer then?"

"I don't know if I'd go that far. Just because it has taken me a long time to figure it out doesn't mean it will take you a long time too. *I* just might have been particularly lost. I will tell you this, and it might save you some time: I'm pretty sure I've eliminated anything that starts with 'I' or 'self.' I'm convinced my identity comes from somewhere or someone. I think it's something I was born with and was bestowed upon me. I've come to believe I cannot begin this search with or within me."

"What's left? Where would I begin?"

"Have you ever been told, or have you ever heard someone tell another person, 'You were made for this?'"

SEASONS

"Sure. There was a girl in my school who was crazy talented with a paint brush and people said that to her all the time."

"The implication is that she had a purpose. That she was born with something unique, something bestowed upon her."

"Right."

"Well, that's where I'm looking to find my identity. If she was made for that, who made her, and why? For that matter, who made me? I think that's where I'll find my identity, not in the things I can do."

"That sounds almost too philosophical for me."

"Maybe this will help. It's a bit dark, but it helped me. Maybe it's because I lost my arm, but I began to wonder, 'What if the accident had been worse?' What if I had been paralyzed? What if I couldn't speak anymore? What if I was totally dependent on someone else? What then?"

"You were right, that is dark. I don't like to think like that."

"I didn't dwell on it. I just tried to define my identity without the use of tasks or abilities to help me. If I was totally dependent, who would I be? I figure when I know that answer, I'll know the answer in general because if it was true of me then, it would be true of me now."

"And you've been thinking about this for how long?"

"Oh, it's been years. But don't let that discourage you. I am a far healthier person today just by eliminating some of the false identities and, like Edison, the more I eliminate, the closer I am to my answer and the healthier I become."

"That's interesting."

"It's kinda fun actually."

IDENTITY

"Laura," Swap said, "I hope you find the answer to your question sooner rather than later, but let me assure you of something: your father loves you regardless of what you do or don't do. You're his little girl and there's nothing you can do to change that."

"Thanks, Swap. I know that. Dad's always been good to me. I'm actually headed over there next. He wasn't excited I was stopping here when I first got to town, so he made me promise I get out to the house as soon as possible. I better get going."

"Thanks for coming by to speak with J. I appreciate it very much," Swap said.

"It was my pleasure," she said, as Swap helped her down from the chair.

"Thanks, Mrs. Thompson. You've got an incredible story and I'm glad you shared it with me."

"I just hope it was in some small way helpful."

"I think it was," I said.

Laura Thompson walked into the smothering heat, got into her car and drove away. I realized, before the conversation was over, I'd stopped noticing her for her missing arm and was just appreciating her as a person. If for nothing else, that made the conversation forever worthwhile.

My stomach was churning, so I asked my grandpa if he was going to let me eat. He reassured me that lunch was on the schedule and that we'd be eating with the next visitor. I was officially eager for him to show up.

DISCUSSION QUESTIONS

1. Laura said she was known as "Laura, the tennis player." Have you ever been so closely associated with your sport that it became a way people identified you? Talk about how it affected you.

2. Talk about any pressure you may have felt from your friends, family or community in relation to your athletic future.

3. We don't like to think about it, but it happens every year, so try this exercise out. Imagine enduring an injury that ended your career in your sport. How do you think you would feel? What do you think you would do? How do you think people would treat you?

4. What do you think the phrases "adoration of praise" and "adoration of sympathy" mean? Why do you think people like receiving both of them? Talk about times when you've seen them lived out.

5. Laura warned against forming your identity from the things that you do before going on to ask: "If I was totally dependent, who would I be?" What do you think about her strategy? How would you go about separating the idea of who you are from what you do?

–chapter seven–

ASKING THE RIGHT QUESTIONS

*I believe that having a spiritual life
is so important in everybody's life.*
– LOU HOLTZ, two-time college football Coach of the Year

*An atheist is a man who watches a
Notre Dame – Southern Methodist University game
and doesn't care who wins.*
– DWIGHT EISENHOWER, 34th President of the United States

SEASONS

"Alright Jeff, we'll be back in about an hour." My grandfather put his tools away and we headed for the door. "You've got the place till we get back. We're going to see Dr. Lewis."

"I'll be fine. You guys enjoy your lunch. If you're gone more than an hour, I'm shaving Henry."

"Good luck with that," my grandpa said, shaking his head.

We stepped out of the shop's conditioned air and into the summer's sticky humidity, which felt like each drop of moisture was tinged with syrup. The sun was directly overhead, bullying away any cloud that even thought about entering the sky. Swap walked over to his truck while I leaned against the wall trying to take advantage of the two inches of shade the gutters provided. My grandpa reached inside his burnt orange beater and grabbed his wallet off the seat. "I still can't believe you do that," I said.

"What, use a wallet?"

"You know what I mean. Why don't you lock your doors, and why do you leave your wallet sitting out for the world to see?"

"I've been around a long time and never had a problem."

"Didn't we just talk about how Reggie stole your car?"

"Yep."

"Wouldn't you call that a problem?"

"I guess some people would. But I got a great friend out of the deal, so I'm good."

"You're a better man than me, Grandpa."

FAITH

"You're better than you realize." My grandpa joined me on the sidewalk and we began our short walk to town. "You're going to like this next guy; he'll make you think."

"That's fine, as long as I get some food in me. Are we going to Nana's?"

"Yep."

A little bell jingled as we walked into Nana's Kitchen, and the unmistakable aroma of sausage and coffee welcomed us. The place always served breakfast and was always crowded. Nana died about ten years ago and her family sold the place, but the new owners were local and didn't change a thing. Everyone in the place looked the same and knew each other; typical Columbia County. But in the back there was a man in a shirt and tie who looked as out of place as a sumo wrestler sitting in a baby pool. He looked to be in his fifties and had frazzled brown hair and a leather briefcase by his chair. My grandfather nodded toward him, "That's your lunch date."

We walked to his table and pulled out our chairs. "Jack," my grandpa said, "this is my grandson, J. J, I want you to meet Dr. Jack Lewis."

I reached out to shake his hand. He did the same. "Nice to know you, J. Can I buy you lunch?"

"That's a question I'll never say 'no' to."

The waitress was one of my classmates. Her parents ran the restaurant and she had been working here since we were in middle school. I flipped the laminated, greasy menu over a few times before ordering the biscuits and gravy with a side of bacon and a chocolate milk. Grandpa ordered two eggs, two link sausages, a piece of toast, and a coffee. Dr. Lewis ordered a western omelet and already had his coffee. He took a sip and said to me, "How's your day going?"

"It's been educational."

"I'm sure it has. We can learn a lot from the experiences of others."

"I suppose. So what's your story?"

"Well, to put it bluntly, I'm here to talk with you about the big questions of life."

My friend brought the coffee and my chocolate milk, "Your food will be out in just a minute."

I thanked her and looked back at Dr. Lewis, "The big questions?"

"Yeah. Questions like 'Why am I here? What's wrong with the world? Is there a God?' Stuff like that."

"I can make the conversation a little shorter."

"How's that?" he asked.

"Because I know why I'm here."

"Do tell."

"Because I'm hungry."

My grandpa smacked me in the back of the head playfully.

"That's why I'm here too, but the 'here' I was referring to is existence. Why do you exist? It's one of life's big questions."

"I'm sure it is, but why mess with it? I've never thought about it and I think I'm doing fine."

"Understanding why something exists helps you understand its purpose. When you understand its purpose, you'll know

FAITH

the correct way to use it. For example, do you know what this is?" He took a pop top from a Coke can out of his pocket.

"Yeah, it's a pop top."

"It was a pop top."

"It still is."

"Okay then, use it."

I looked at the little piece of aluminum and back to Dr. Lewis, "I guess I can't"

"That's because it's not a pop top."

"Then what is it?"

"It's a duck call."

I wasn't much of a hunter myself, but I'd been around hunters my whole life and I'd seen plenty of duck calls. This was no duck call. "That's not a duck call."

"Sure it is." He was dead serious.

"Okay then, use it."

He picked the object up, held it to his lips and said, "Here ducky, ducky, ducky. Here ducky, ducky, ducky."

"You've got to be kidding me," I said, and then looked at my grandpa. His shoulders were bouncing as he laughed in his coffee mug. Dr. Lewis grinned like a Disney character. Thankfully, my friend arrived with our food. I shook my head at the goofy men and took a bite of my bacon. With my mouth still a little full I said, "You guys are a couple of clowns."

"He's as brilliant a man as you'll ever meet," my grandpa said, "but he's one of a kind for sure."

"Thanks, Swap." Dr. Lewis began eating his omelet and between bites continued the conversation. "Like I was saying, understanding something's purpose allows you to use it correctly. A better example would be to think about needing to unscrew a screw. To do it, you need to know the purpose for the different tools in a tool box. A hammer is great, but not for loosening a screw. Just like a screwdriver is great until you want to saw a board in half. Intelligent beings design things for a specific purpose and using them appropriately sure makes life easier."

"Well sure, I get that."

"I knew you did. Most people readily accept the relationship between design and purpose when it comes to tools, or engine parts, or sporting goods. However, when you start to think about things like people, relationships, and consequences, many people don't think about them in the context of design and purpose."

"I guess I can see that too. I've never thought about that stuff before. Well, I guess I've wondered about my purpose in life, but I've never spent a lot of time on it."

"Most young people never do. The older we get, and as our relational titles grow to things like spouse and parent, the more we think about these questions, but because many people think about them so late, they carry a lot of regret into the process. For example, in an effort to climb the professional ladder someone might have used and manipulated people to reach the top only to look back one day and realize they're lonely, the friends they thought they had resent them, and they barely recognize their kids. By the time they accept they had their priorities out of order, they have a history of regret."

FAITH

"It's not really the same," I said, "but one of my friends decided he wanted to play ball in college, but didn't think about it until he was a senior. But by then his grades kept him from seriously considering one of the big schools. He didn't get any offers, even though he's a good player, so he's trying to enroll in a junior college."

"That's a perfect example. How different would he have behaved if he had college ball on his radar as a freshman? There is a difference though; your example is asking the question, 'What do I want to do?' where I'm talking about the bigger question, 'Why do we exist in the first place?'"

"Where do you find an answer to a question like that?" I finished my bacon and loaded my fork with a bite of gravy-soaked biscuit my mom would never have let me put in my mouth at one time."

"That sort of depends on whom you ask. Were you to ask an atheist — someone who believes there is absolutely no God — he would answer the question from a purely biological perspective. His answer will involve living for self and competing with others, because it's the root concept of survival of the fittest. However, if you were to ask a theist — someone who believes there is a god — he would answer from a spiritual perspective. He may talk of things like loving others or serving a higher power."

"How would you answer the question?"

"That's the wrong question."

"Then what's the right question?"

"The right question is: 'How do I answer the question?'"

"That's what I said. How would you answer the question?"

"No. I mean how would *you* answer the question." He pointed a forkful of eggs and green pepper at me. "I'm not here to give you answers. I'm here to get you to think about the right questions. The purpose question leads to the bigger question about the existence or nonexistence of God. Do you believe in God?"

"I guess so; I've been around the church a long time."

"Belief in God and participation in church are not the same thing. Try to answer the question without using church."

"I don't know. I think I've always believed there is a god."

"So do you believe in God, or do you believe there is a god?"

"What the difference?"

"That's a good question. The agnostic believes there might or might not be a god, but is reluctant to say absolutely either way. Where the theist believes both that there is a god and that God can be known. The different religious groups are based on theistic beliefs."

"So I just need to pick a religion?"

"No, not at all. What is the right religion is the wrong question. How you choose to worship is based on how you answer the God question, not the other way around. Religion is an expression of belief, not the object of belief. Plus, not all religions answer the God question the same way."

"You mean like how Christians and Muslims believe in different gods?"

"Not exactly. Those two religions express belief in similar ways and answer the God question in similar ways, even though they have different answers. I'm talking about the difference between say the Jewish faith system, the Hindu faith system, and *Avatar*."

"The movie?"

"Yeah. You'll see what I mean. The Old Testament of the Bible is shared by the Christian, Muslim, and Jewish faiths for example. Generally speaking, these religions are monotheistic. Monotheism is just a big word that means belief in one God. The Hindu faith is polytheistic which simply means belief in multiple gods. Greek and Roman mythology were expressions of polytheism. In *Avatar*, those big blue guys held a pantheistic view of their world. They believed that God is in everything and more of an essence than a knowable entity. If you've looked at Native American culture very much, you've seen pantheistic ideas. *Star Wars* is another example of pantheism. The Jedi are deep pantheists, calling their god 'The Force.'"

"If I don't need to pick a religion, why are you telling me about these different religions?"

"I'm simply trying to show you all religions aren't the same. That's why your question cannot be which religion is best. Remember, religion is an expression of belief, not the object of belief."

"I'm trying, but I don't think I see the difference."

"You said you grew up around the church, right?"

"Yeah."

"I'm assuming you mean a Christian church?"

"Yep."

"But when I asked if you believed in God you weren't sure."

"Right."

"See, you are a perfect example of someone expressing what I call cultural faith. You've participated in the popular religion of your area but never really considered what you believe. You've passively believed in a religion without really considering what the religion claims to believe."

"You're saying the fact I've been to church doesn't mean I believe in God?"

"Exactly. But taking it a bit further, many people assume belief in God because they go to church, or people assume another person believes in God because that person goes to a church. Neither conclusion is necessarily correct."

"Are you saying I shouldn't go to church?"

"No, I'm not saying that either. I am saying don't assume an individual's attendance in a religious service equates to belief in what they worship. You can learn a lot from attending, but you still have to answer the God question for yourself."

"What if someone doesn't believe in God?"

"The same is true for them. They still have a religion and still worship; they just keep their faith on the ground level. Their holy book is a scientific textbook. Their religion's leaders are the biologists and cosmologists of history and today. The theist might quote Moses whereas the atheist might quote Darwin, but in either case they are putting their faith in something they find believable. I would challenge the atheist to answer the God question too. I've come across very few authentic atheists in my day, atheists who have really thought about it

FAITH

and examined the evidence. Most "atheists" have the same cultural faith you expressed. They've always been around atheistic ideas, but they've never really explored them."

"So, how do I explore the God question?"

"I would encourage you to talk to authentic believers, read their sacred books, and examine the evidence."

"The evidence?"

"Yeah, look around you. A caterpillar becomes a butterfly; that's evidence of something. The question is what."

"Is that how you started, with the caterpillar?"

"No. I was a little more simplistic. I began with conclusions. The atheist believes when we die we're just fertilizer. The theist believes when we die there's something else. I figured if the atheist was right I have nothing to lose and can explore its claims in time. But if the theist was right I needed to get some answers pretty quick. So I began my search as an agnostic I guess."

"But doesn't science explain how everything got here? Doesn't the evidence prove there is no god?"

"Look at that, you're as much a cultural atheist as you are a cultural theist. You claim to believe in God and not believe in God at the same time." Dr. Lewis cocked his head and looked at me over the top of his glasses, "I'm not sure either club would accept you." He picked up his cup to take a drink and paused before it reached his mouth. "But to your statement, the atheist has no proof of God's existence or nonexistence. He puts faith in the theories articulated in his sacred books, the textbooks. But no matter how sophisticated the explanation, ultimately the theorists weren't there, so it comes down to faith. The Christian, as an alternative example, believes God created the world and cites the Bible as his source. Most scholars say Moses wrote Genesis, but he wasn't there when the world began either, so we have very similar examples and both require faith." He brought the cup to his lips and drank his coffee.

"But isn't the Bible less reliable than a textbook? It's an old book and I don't even know who wrote it? Why would I believe it?"

"First of all, I'm not telling you to believe it. Second, do you know who wrote your science book?"

"No."

"Then why do you believe it? J, you're on the right track, but you're coming to your conclusions a bit too soon. Let me ask you this, do you believe we landed on the moon?"

"Absolutely."

"Can you prove it? Were you there?"

"I wasn't there, but someone was and they wrote about it."

"Okay, what are your sources? Are they reliable?"

"I guess my sources are my school books and maybe my parents. They said it happened. And I would consider my parents reliable."

"Fair enough, I consider my parents reliable too. But do you consider everyone's parents reliable? Are parents a historically trustworthy source? I'm sure you've seen *The Waterboy*. Would you consider Bobby Boucher's mama a trustworthy source?"

"I guess not, but what about the textbooks? I think they're reliable."

"Why do you think that? Have you ever examined them for mistakes? Do you know anything about the authors or publishers?"

"I've never thought about it."

"And that's exactly what I want you to do, think about it. Now I'm not saying textbooks are bad or you should discount everything in them. I am saying you should put both sets of the religious texts – the sacred and the scientific – through the same scrutiny."

"I don't really know what scrutiny I put the Bible through; how could I do the same to my school books?"

"You asked earlier, 'Isn't the Bible less reliable than a textbook?'"

"Yes I did."

"So for some reason you doubt the integrity of the Bible, but not of the textbooks, or at least not as much. Would that be correct?"

"I suppose."

"And you're not alone; a lot of people struggle to accept the content of the Bible. But what we tend to do is transfer our struggles with the Bible's content and place them on the Bible's reliability."

I almost had another bite, but had to ask to interrupt, "What do you mean?"

"Many people find some of the content in the Bible hard to believe, stuff like the miracles or some of the moral claims.

SEASONS

Because they struggle believing the content, they assume the book itself must be unreliable. Imagine a ninety-year-old woman sitting across the table from Bill Gates listening to him explain operating systems. Because she can't begin to understand what he was saying, she writes him off as loony, although we both know he might be the most reliable computer guy on the planet."

"I see now."

"You might reject the content in the Bible, but you'd be a fool to reject its reliability."

"Why do you say that?"

"Have you ever doubted what is said or written about Plato or Caesar?"

"No. But I've never read them either."

"Fair enough, but I want you to consider a couple things. Caesar's book, *Gallic Wars*, was written sometime between 100 and 44 B.C., and the earliest copies we have of the text are dated around 900 A.D., so there's roughly one thousand years between when it was written and the earliest copy we have."

"That's a long time."

"It sure is, plenty of time for transcription errors or complete fallacy to show up."

"Fallacy?"

"It's a word used in logic, but basically it refers to something incorrect or illogical."

"Got it."

"Okay. So there's a thousand years separating its writing and our copies, but we do have ten copies available to cross check, which adds to the reliability of the text."

"Why is that?"

"If we come across a claim that seems a bit off, we can look for it in the other nine copies. If it exists in all of them we can feel more confident about its inclusion in the original text. We can still be skeptical of the claim, but we don't doubt its reliability. Are you following?"

"Yeah, so far."

"Good. Now our confidence in Plato's work is even shakier. His work dates at 400 B.C., but of the seven copies we have, the earliest also dates to 900 A.D. That's thirteen hundred years. But even with that span of time, we generally believe what we have is reliable."

"Okay ..."

"Now consider the New Testament, the final quarter or so of the Bible. It was written between 50 and 100 A.D. The earliest manuscript we have of the entire thing dates to 325 A.D., and we have fragments dated as early as 114 A.D. Worst case scenario, there's only two hundred twenty-five years spanning the original and our first copies."

"Wait, why would there be like nine hundred years for Caesar but only one or two hundred for the New Testament?"

"There are a few reasons for that: motivation of the believers to protect it, availability of writing materials, amount of literate people, and so on. But that's beside the point. The point is we don't doubt the reliability, generally speaking, of those other works, yet we doubt the Bible. Don't you find that interesting?"

"Actually, I do. How many copies of the New Testament are there?"

"I'm glad you asked. There are ten copies of Caesar's *Gallic Wars* and seven copies of Plato's work, but we *only* have five thousand three hundred sixty-six copies of the New Testament."

"That's a lot of Bibles."

"Not whole Bibles mind you, just copies of the New Testament. But you're right; there are a lot of them. Let me read you something." Dr. Lewis pulled one of those notepads of yellow paper from his briefcase and read from it. "This was said by Sir Frederic G. Kenyon, who was the principal librarian of the British Museum and considered by many as the authority on manuscripts. He said, and I quote, 'The interval, then, between the dates of the original composition and the earliest extant evidence becomes so small as to be in fact negligible, and the last foundation for any doubt that the Scriptures have come down to us substantially as they were written has now been removed. Both the authenticity and the general integrity of the books of the New Testament may be regarded as finally established.' In other words, what we read today is what was written originally."

"You're telling me I should feel more confident about the reliability of the Bible than I do about other books from history?"

FAITH

"I believe that, but I'm not necessarily saying that. I'm simply saying you need to be consistent in your criticism, and if you're going to question the reliability of one you need to know why and apply the same logic across the board."

"That sounds fair, but the Bible still has some pretty crazy stuff in it. It's hard to believe."

"Oh there's no doubt about that. Every major religion in the world has sacred books and most, if not all of them, have miraculous claims in them. The Old Testament alone, a book shared by Jewish, Muslim, and Christian faiths, includes pillars of fire from the sky, seas parting, donkeys and snakes talking, the dead being raised to life, bread falling from Heaven, and all kinds of other astounding accounts. This is where faith comes in."

"Well, I guess I struggle having faith then."

"You aren't alone there either. Shoot, the guys that ran around with Jesus struggled to maintain faith. Believing in something you cannot see, especially something that claims to accomplish unexplainable things, isn't easy."

"But I suppose you believe?"

"I'll tell you this; I believe the universe is far too big, far too specific, and far too beautiful to be totally left to chance. And I also believe we know far too little to absolutely rule out the existence of God. I also believe the Bible, and the New Testament specifically, is the most historically reliable sacred text the world has even known. How about that?"

"I'd say you believe."

"Okay, but remember the most important question."

"And that is?"

"Do you believe?" Dr. Lewis let the question hang as he gathered his stuff. He reached for the check but Swap grabbed it first, left some cash on the table, stood up, and said, "Well, Doc, you've certainly given us some things to think about."

"Just promise me you'll actually do it."

"Do what?" I asked, rising to stand beside them.

"Think about our conversation. If you want to reject the Bible, or any book or idea, that's up to you, but make sure you know what you're rejecting. Far too many people dismiss things before ever really understanding them, and even fewer consider the consequences of their actions. I'd encourage you to be more thoughtful."

"We'll do just that," Swap said, and he led us back through Nana's. I said goodbye to my waitress friend as we walked outside.

"Thanks for lunch, Swap." Dr. Lewis extended his hand.

"Are you kidding?" Swap shook his hand with a big smile. "It was our pleasure. I appreciate your time."

"Yeah, thanks Dr. Lewis. I promise to give all this some thought."

"Good to know. You gentlemen have a nice afternoon." He climbed into a midnight blue sedan and drove away. We turned the other direction and headed back to the barber shop with way more than just food to digest.

DISCUSSION QUESTIONS

1. Dr. Lewis made the connection between an object's design and its purpose. When we look at a fork lift or a helicopter we accept that relationship, but many people struggle with the design and purpose relationship when it comes to people. Why do you think that is?

2. Why do you think the question of purpose is so closely connected to the question of God's existence?

3. If someone were considering the existence of God Dr. Lewis said their "questions cannot be which religion is best," because "religion is an expression of belief, not the object of belief." Do you agree with that assessment? Why or why not?

4. What did you think of Dr. Lewis' idea of "cultural faith" – someone who passively claims a belief without really considering that belief's implications? Have you ever seen examples of this "cultural faith?" Do you think there could be a relationship between people with "cultural faith" and the belief that religious people are hypocrites?

5. What did you think about the discussion involving text books and the Bible?

6. One of Dr. Lewis' closing statements was, "If you want to reject the Bible, or any book or idea, that's up to you, but make sure you know what you're rejecting. Far too many people dismiss things before ever really understanding them, and even fewer consider the consequences of their actions." What do you think about this challenge?

— chapter eight —

TRUSTING THE PROCESS

*On this team, we're all united
in a common goal: to keep my job.*
— LOU HOLTZ, 2008 College Football Hall of Fame inductee

*Gentlemen, it is better to have died
as a small boy than to fumble this football.*
— JOHN HEISMAN, 1954 College Football Hall of Fame inductee

*Basketball is a team game.
But that doesn't mean all five players
should have the same amount of shots.*
— DEAN SMITH, 2006 College Basketball Hall of Fame inductee

SEASONS

I FELT LIKE I'D JUST PUT IN an all-night cram session. The walk back to Swap's Shop was much needed after all that talking and all that eating. The food from Nana's stays with you for a while. Grandpa tossed his wallet back through his window onto the driver's seat. I've been tempted to hide it many, many times, but for some reason I can't bring myself to do it. He probably wouldn't even say anything about it. The next time I saw him he'd have a new wallet and still be leaving it in his unlocked car.

"I hope my next guest is a little easier than my last one."

"I doubt Terry will be as particular, but he'll sure 'nuff make you think."

Slobber ran up to us as we walked into the shop. Jeff was nowhere to be seen, but there was a man sitting, looking at his phone when we walked in. Grandpa didn't seem too concerned, but he also leaves his wallet sitting out. I could tell what this man did for a living the moment I saw him. He was in school-issued cross trainers, red athletic pants, and a Gatehawks baseball T-shirt. Our little town was built on top of an old Civil War camp and the only remaining evidence is a stone gate near the tiny college campus. There's always been a family of hawks that called that gate home, so the Gatehawk idea was born to honor our past and recognize the present. I think it's pretty cool.

His face was mostly hidden behind the bill of his black Gatehawks hat and his phone, but it was obvious the man was a coach. I've considered becoming a coach when I'm done playing almost purely because of the clothes they get to wear. All the adults in my school have to wear stuffy clothes with

COACHES

collars and church shoes, but coaches are in sweats, T-shirts and Nike shoes – that's my kind of uniform.

"How you doing, Terry?" My grandpa walked to the man's chair.

"You know me," said the coach, putting away his phone, "even if we lose twenty to nothin', I'm still gettin' paid to coach ball so I'm good." The men shook hands. "Where's Jeff?"

"I was about to ask you the same thing," Swap said.

"The store was empty when I got here, except for that lazy old dog."

"J, would you try to find your uncle while I get Mr. Hill ready for his cut?"

My finger slid over the screen, forty-four, forty-four — my football number twice — and the phone unlocked. I sent Jeff a quick text, *"Grandpa's looking for you. The shop was robbed."* When I dropped into the chair next to the coach I felt about ten pounds heavier from lunch.

"Did you get him?"

"I texted him."

"Call him, please. These kids and their texting." He looked to the coach for support but found him finishing a text himself.

"Sorry, Swap." He was laughing. "One of my assistants had a question."

Jeff's phone was already ringing in my ear. He had the worst ringbacks. I was listening to some synthesized '80s junk, *"Take on me. Take me on."* Thankfully, Jeff didn't let the guys finish. "Hey, J, nice text."

SEASONS

"How can you listen to that garbage?"

"Listen to what garbage?"

"The stuff you call music on your ringback."

"You wouldn't know good music if it introduced itself to you and gave you an ID."

"If that's what you call good music, I wouldn't want to. Where are you?"

"I had to run home and bring the wife my keys; she'd locked hers in the car. I'm already driving back, that's why I didn't respond to your text."

"You know you left the shop unlocked?"

"Sure. We do it all the time."

"You guys are crazy. See you later."

I slid my phone back in my pocket. "Jeff's on his way. His wife locked herself out of her car and he ran keys home to her. The man leaves your store unlocked in the middle of the day, but his wife locks her car in their driveway. Can someone explain that to me?"

"I stopped trying to explain for Jeff a long time ago." My grandpa had the coach all set up for his hair cut, and now that I could see his face, I recognized him. "J, this is Terry Hill."

I reached over to shake his hand, but he just nodded to me.

"Oh yeah, sorry." I pulled my hand back, realizing how dumb it was to try to shake his hand while he had it hidden beneath the barber cloth. "It's nice to meet you sir."

Coach Hill was kind of a big deal around here. The second year he was the coach, the Gatehawks set a record for the most wins in a season, and he'd broken that record the last

COACHES

two years. He hadn't won it all though, and he may not get to because bigger schools have been looking at him. The locals hope his connection to the program is enough for him to stick around. He played third base for the college about fifteen years ago.

"It's good to meet you, son. I hear you're headed up to State on a football scholarship."

"Yessir, that's right."

"That's good, real good. I'm afraid I don't follow football too closely though. Most Saturdays I'm out on the diamond working on the field."

"I thought there was a grounds crew that did that."

"Oh there is. They cut the grass and keep the stadium in order, but I just love being out there. I'll rake around the bases or line the field; it helps me think."

"Are you here to talk to me about taking care of my things?"

"No." His face turned real serious, brow furrowed, eyes almost squinting, "I'm here to talk to you about coaches."

"Coaches?"

"Yep. Swap thought it would be a good idea for you to hear about things from our perspective, and I couldn't agree more. You know what the secret is to being a great shortstop?"

"Ah, no."

"Know what the pitcher's throwing."

"Well yeah, if I knew what pitch was coming I would crush the ball too."

"I'm not talking about hitting, son. I mean in the field. The best shortstops know what their pitcher's about to throw and adjust accordingly. If there's a righty in the box and they know an outside fast ball is on the way, they inch ever so slightly toward second. It makes all the difference. Occasionally a batter will surprise them, but the odds are against it."

I looked at him, waiting for him to tell me why we were talking about shortstops.

"The point is, understanding what the other person is doing makes the whole team better. The same is true for players and coaches. If my guys understand me and how I operate, we all do much better. Sometimes it takes the guys a few months, maybe a year to figure things out, but once they do, we gel. You're getting a head start on that process."

"I'm all about head starts. What do I need to know?"

"Number one: he's in charge, period. One of the toughest things my freshmen seem to struggle with is submitting to my authority. That's my diamond. Standing on it is a privilege. I'm betting your coach feels the same way about that ball field."

"Obviously. I know he's in charge."

"Yeah, you think you do. But what happens when he changes something in your stance or form that you've been successful with for years? What then? I can't tell you how many times I've had players who simply wouldn't listen when I tried to tweak their throwing motion or adjust their hands in their swing."

"They tell you no?"

"No. Very few are as bold as that. They just won't do it. Part of it is breaking a habit, but a bigger part of it is trust."

COACHES

"I thought we were talking about submitting to your authority?"

"We are, and submitting to authority is all about trust. Initially, players will submit because I'm the coach. They've been listening to coaches their whole life. But eventually I'll ask them to do something that's different from what they're used to. At that point, it's about trust. If they trust me, they'll do it. If they don't, they won't. But if they don't, they won't play either. Remember, it's my diamond."

"That still just sounds like doing what I'm told."

"Have you ever seen any of those boot camp, military movies?"

"A couple maybe, why?"

"Because Boot Camp is all about trust; trusting the system, trusting your superior officer, trusting your fellow man. When new guys show up, they enter a grueling, humbling world of commands, some simple to understand, some that appear quite unorthodox. But none of the commands are about the specific task necessarily; they are about developing absolute submission motivated by absolute trust. Reason being, when those men enter a battle, they must trust. Their life depends on it."

"But we're talking about sports. No one's life is on the line."

"Granted, but the principle remains. Often, young soldiers hate their drill sergeant, and rightly so. His purpose requires him to drive his men to their limits. But once they get to the other side and begin to understand what it was all for, they grow to love that man. They see how little they knew and appreciate what he taught them. But deep down, that trust was there all along. The guys that can't trust, the ones trying to get through on pure willpower, they are the ones who drop out."

"But how do they trust a guy they've never met?"

"That's where trusting the system comes in. You've met your coach obviously, but you've only known him as a recruit. When you get on the field, everything changes, but I'll get to that in a minute. If they're like me, they will spend the early part of your training breaking all the bad habits you developed in high school. No offense to your high school coaches, but no matter how good they are, they likely don't teach the same technique your college coaches will. And coaches are particular about doing things their way. Even guys that play ball for elite college programs, when they get to the pros, their new coaches do the same thing. And there's a deeply personal reason for that, but I'll get to that later too. When they start telling you to change your stance, alter your tackling form, run differently, whatever, you have to trust they know what they're talking about, and trust they actually care about your development. Until you get to know them, look at what they've accomplished. They win games and they develop players, otherwise they'd be unemployed. Let your trust for what they've done push you to do what they ask."

"Sounds simple enough."

"And it is, if you learn to trust. If you're doing it begrudgingly, what they tell you won't stick and you'll fall back into your old habits."

COACHES

"I think I can do that."

"You can." My grandpa looked me in the eyes. "You've always had a coachable spirit and a willing heart. Besides, it sure seemed like you and the coach up at State got along fine."

"Yeah, he's pretty cool."

Coach Hill laughed. "We're all pretty cool, during recruiting. We're on our best behavior trying to convince you, your mom and dad, your best friend, and your girlfriend to commit the next four or five years of your life to us. We laugh at your jokes, tell you how great you are, and make sure you know our program might not survive if you don't rescue us. But once you sign that paper, son, it all changes. We're still the same person, but you might not think so. Your coaches will start to treat you completely different, because their goals have changed. In recruiting, they are trying to get you to come play for them. On the field, they are trying to win games and make you better. Your jokes aren't funny anymore."

"I kinda figured that."

"Well, it will be worse than you think, so get ready for it. Just remember, you're not a recruit anymore. Now you're part of the team with a job to do. Now you have responsibilities and expectations. But while we're on the recruiting process, let me add one more thing. You're a little beyond this, but you can still let it sink in; you didn't commit to a coach, you committed to a school. Your coach could be gone tomorrow. Maybe he gets fired, maybe another school comes calling, or maybe the pros give him a shot. Either way, the man who recruited you can be coaching you on Monday and packing his office tomorrow. You need to realize you are now part of a university, part of a huge network of people. You can't waver if your coach doesn't stay with you. Maybe it won't affect you, but maybe it will. Just be prepared to adapt and keep playing ball."

"I can understand if he got fired, and I guess I get it if he went to 'the show,' but how am I to trust my coach if I know he may bolt for another team the first chance he gets?"

"That's a fair question, but you have to understand one very big difference between you and your coach — you're in college and he's providing for himself and his family."

"Why is that so important?"

"Because you're playing a game; he's going to work every day. Your coach will have to make choices that hurt people, like putting a player he really likes on the bench because the sophomore behind him is more productive. He might have to fire a coach he considers a friend because things aren't working out on the field. While you're at your apartment playing your Xbox, he's sacrificing time with his kids because he feels he needs to get the team prepared for the next game. H has fifteen recruits to call or he is on a plane to Maryland to tell some teenager how great he is. Son, to put it bluntly, he's a grown man making grown man decisions. You're in college having the time of your life."

Being talked to like a child isn't cool, but for some reason it didn't bother me with Coach Hill. He had nothing to gain by talking to me, except maybe a free haircut, and he seemed to be speaking from the heart, so I gave him the benefit of

COACHES

the doubt. "Assuming that's true, it's still going to be hard to trust him if he may run out on us."

"Didn't you hear what I said to you?"

"Yeah. You said he has to provide for his family so he may take a different job."

"And that's true, but think about it for a minute. If your job was on the line, providing for your family and all that, would you short change the players who would determine whether you kept that job? If you were trying to get noticed by some other team, wouldn't you want the kids you coached to be performing at their highest levels, exceeding expectations? Wouldn't you want to win every game you coached?"

"Of course."

"That's why you can trust him. This may sound terribly selfish, but you can trust him because he's got his own best interest in mind. I'm not talking about men who lack character here, that's not the kind of best interest I'm referring to. I'm talking about coaches who will give you everything they have because they want to win as bad as you do. These are guys who would keep their nephew on the bench if the other guy helps them win. They can't afford to play favorites with players or coaches, because the moment they do is the moment they lose their job."

"It does sound selfish. But it makes sense too. It's kind of the same for me I guess. My coach will use my desire to win or advance my career to get me to do things I don't want to do I suppose. And he will trust all of us to do what we're asked, banking on the idea that we want to win."

"Exactly. The trick for both you and the coach is to realize putting the team first allows you to succeed as an individual, but purely putting yourself first hurts both the individual and the team. Those low character guys don't get it and hurt everybody. But people who have integrity do what it takes for the team to succeed and end up accomplishing their goals along the way."

"That works for me."

"But it is a double-edged sword. If you're doing what you're supposed to do, things will be fine. But if you do something stupid, the sword of self-preservation is coming for you. One of the last things I say to my guys before a weekend or a long break is, 'Don't make me look bad,' and I mean it. Because if they make me look bad, I have to answer for it, and if I have to answer for it, you better believe they will have to as well. If your foolishness puts your coach's job at risk, don't be surprised if he returns the favor. He's not going to lose his job to protect an immature kid who can't stay out of the clubs."

"I can respect that. I've actually felt the same way when I've had teammates act stupid and hurt our chances. It's just not worth it to me."

"That's good to hear, son, good to hear."

"Terry, I can attest to J's no-nonsense attitude when it comes to off-the-field stuff." Swap stopped cutting for a moment. "He's had his future in front of him for a long time, and he makes choices in light of it. I know you have to get back to the school, so would share your 'Four Ps' with J before you go?"

COACHES

"Four Ps?" I asked, curious to know what this could be about.

The Coach's eyes lit up. "You know I will, Swap. J, a leader on my team must exhibit the Four Ps. It doesn't matter where he is on the depth chart or what year he is, just so long as he lives these values. The Ps are: *Priority, Process, Positive,* and *Presence.* Let me tell you what they mean."

"Please do," I said, proud of my corny use of another P word.

"A leader must be committed to the priority. He has to put the team first. And he must understand his coach's priorities and help enforce them. One of my priorities, for example, is that my guys sprint to first base no matter how hard they hit the ball. You never know what could happen, and a ninety-foot sprint is good for them anyway. My guys know this is a big deal for me, so when one of the veterans sees a young guy pull up short or loaf out of the box, they'll jump all over that kid. They're enforcing my priorities, and that's a must for me. These guys identify the cancers in the locker room and address them. If a kid has a lazy work ethic or a bad attitude, these guys coach 'em up. They're committed to the priority."

"Even as a freshman? Would you want a new kid correcting an upperclassman?"

"Sure. But the challenge with the young kids is to know if they're really committed to the priority or just trying to impress the coach. Some guys come in thinking they're the greatest player since Willie Mays and it shows up when they talk to people. Don't be that guy. The way you address another player is actually one of the other Ps, but it's not the next one."

"My bad, what's the next one?"

"One of my leaders must affirm the process. He has to understand the philosophy that drives our team. We are a pitching, defense, small-ball kind of baseball team. I don't need a bunch of guys swinging for the fences all the time. They have to understand and affirm the process, even if that means they sacrifice. They have to be able to know the difference between short term success and long term victory. A young kid might have terrible technique but still make a flashy play; that's short term success. And for a moment we'll celebrate the out, but making the play doesn't excuse him from learning and living the correct technique. You see what I mean?"

"Absolutely. Holding might give the appearance that a lineman is doing his job, but it won't make him better in the long run. I get that."

"Good. Then the third P deals with how you talk to someone. One of my leaders must be positive with people. There is a way to correct someone without being negative. My leaders will tell a guy his actions or attitudes are wrong, but they won't degrade him. Publically, we speak praise. Privately, we provide correction. We don't blame teammates or coaches for the team's failures. So in your example, a young guy could pull the upperclassman aside to avoid showing him up or showing off and remind him of the process. That's a lot different than trying to embarrass him in front of his teammates. Our guys must be positive with people."

"That one's important, J," my grandpa said. "They're all important, but that one's special to me. So many problems

COACHES

could be avoided just by applying that rule. At the end of the day, or career, it's people that matter, so treat each of them with dignity." He paused for a moment and then went back to taking the barber cloth off Coach Hill.

"And the last P," the coach said, "is presence, and it's twofold. One of my leaders must stay in the game, figuratively and literally. Athletes tend to be pretty competitive, and that's fine, but they also must have a cooperative spirit as well. I can't have guys checking out on their team just because they don't start or get pulled from a game. Neither can they mope and pout if they make a bad play. We need every guy focused on the job at hand and every guy encouraging the others along the way. If one of my guys is in the dugout or on the field, but isn't present mentally, they'll find themselves in the locker room. When that game or practice is over, I'll mince no words explaining to that young man how his attitude is corrosive and absolutely will not be tolerated. They don't get to make that mistake twice either, because if the only example you provide is a bad one, you won't be setting that example for long, at least not on my diamond. This second component is really about off-the-field issues more than playing time. My role players are great leaders, even though they have limited playing time. But if a kid is not making his grades a priority, or does something to make me look bad, he will cease to have a presence on my ball team. It's really just that simple."

"So you're saying if I'm committed to the priority, affirming of the process, and positive with people and present, I'll be successful?"

SEASONS

"Without hesitation, just so long as you know being a success doesn't necessarily mean being a superstar. Remember, even role players are leaders and are successful."

"Yep, I get that. That's good stuff, Coach."

"Thanks." He let a little grin escape. "I've already started working with Tim Miller to get it into book form." He laughed, and Swap laughed with him. While they were laughing, the store's bell dinged and Jeff walked in.

"What's so funny? What'd I miss?"

"Nothing," Swap said. "Did you rescue your bride?"

"Yeah, she's fine. Crisis averted."

"Hey, Jeff," Coach said, "sorry to run out on you, but I have a meeting in fifteen minutes. Give my best to your family."

"No problem. I'm sorry I missed you. I'll just do your cut next time."

"Well, I don't know about that." He smacked Jeff on the back as he and Swap laughed. "J, it was great to talk to you, thanks for letting me be a part of your life. I really wish you all the best."

"No, thank you, Coach. I really appreciate your time." And I really did.

"It was my pleasure. Hey, make sure y'all come over to the field and see my boys play. They're gonna be good this year."

With that, he was out the door, jogging to his truck.

DISCUSSION QUESTIONS

1. What do you think about the following statement from Coach Hill? "One of the toughest things my freshmen seem to struggle with is submitting to my authority. That's my diamond. Standing on it is a privilege."

2. Coach Hill established a relationship between submission to authority and trust of the person in authority. Do you think that makes sense? If you don't trust the person in authority do you think that permits you to ignore or disobey what they ask? Why or why not?

3. Are you going to be surprised if your coach treats you differently as a player than you were treated as a recruit? Obviously a coach isn't going to yell at you and accuse you of being lazy while he's sitting on your couch eating your mom's homemade dessert, but you'll likely hear it one or two times out on the field. Does that mean your coach is two-faced? Do you think it means your coach was lying to you in recruiting and doesn't feel the same way about you as a player? Why or why not?

SEASONS

4. One of the quotes at the beginning of the chapter was from Lou Holtz: "On this team, we're all united in a common goal: to keep my job." Coach Hill elaborated on that idea when he spoke of the real world responsibilities the coach carries. Do think it's fair to ask you to trust your coach when it's possible he or she might take another position? Why or why not?

5. What did you think about Coach Hill's "Four P's" - Priority, Process, Positive, and Presence? Which one do you think is the most important? Which one would you find the toughest to maintain?

—chapter nine—

THE WISE AND THE FOOLS

*In the end, we will remember not
the words of our enemies,
but the silence of our friends.*
— MARTIN LUTHER KING, civil rights activist

*Son, you've got a good engine,
but your hands aren't on the steering wheel.*
— BOBBY BOWDEN, 2006 College Football Hall of Fame inductee

SEASONS

After Coach Hill was gone, Swap flipped the sign on the door to "closed" and began rapidly cleaning up the shop. Jeff grabbed a rag and some kind of spray and wiped down all the seats before cleaning the visible parts of the wall-to-wall mirror. Once the floor was swept and the counters organized, Swap grabbed one of the waiting chairs and moved it a little closer to the barber chairs, right between the second and third seat. I didn't know what was going on so I sat down and scratched Slobber's big head.

"Don't do that, J," my grandpa spoke quickly, but not in anger, "I don't want his hair floating around the store. Take him and lock him in the bathroom please, and set a little bowl of water in there so he doesn't drink out of the toilet."

"Okay." I wasn't sure what to make of all that was happening, but did what Swap told me to do. As soon as Slobber got into the bathroom, his little stub tail started wiggling as he circled the floor. In seconds he found whatever he was looking for and flopped himself onto the cool tile, spreading all four of his legs out beside him. I grinned at his simple contentment, set the bowl in the corner, closed the lid of the toilet, and closed the door as I walked back out to the shop.

"Thanks, J. Mrs. Stanford has some pretty brutal allergies, so we're trying to make the place as safe as possible." My grandfather spoke without taking his eyes off the shelf of baseball memorabilia he was dusting.

"Who is Mrs. Stanford?"

DECISIONS

"She's actually someone I know, J," Jeff said. "Her son and I went to high school together. Swap wanted me to ask her and her husband to come down today."

"Did their son play something in college?"

"I think I'll let them tell the story," he said, wiping the glass cleaner off the front door.

The guys had the store clean in less than ten minutes. While we waited on the Stanfords, Swap told me the extra chair was for me, which I figured already, and Jeff had us fill him in on what Coach Hill talked about. About fifteen minutes later, right as the bells of St. James, the ancient church down the street, started to play, the couple walked in. It was two o'clock in the afternoon.

"Hi, Don. Hi, Erica. Thank you for coming down today," Swap said, shaking each of their hands.

Jeff walked up and gave each of them a hug. "I really appreciate your willingness to come talk to J like this," he said.

"It's an honor, Jeff." Mr. Stanford was tall but appeared even taller because he was so thin. He had a black beard that had grayed around his chin, and gray and black hair on his head. He dressed just like my dad, jeans and a golf shirt, and had a big ring on his right hand that looked a lot like the class ring I had sitting on my shelf back home.

"We actually enjoy talking about it, it helps." Mrs. Stanford had a soft, sweet voice that reminded me of the pediatrician I used to see as a kid. Her hair was fully gray, but she had a lot of it. Part of it was hanging down while part of it was pulled up on the back of her head. She looked like she would

SEASONS

be as comfortable over a stove as she would be in a courtroom. Her blue eyes glistened, slightly watering as she spoke to Jeff and my grandfather. I got the feeling this was going to be a heavy conversation, but I was dying to know what it was about at the same time. Mr. Stanford took his wife's hand and helped her climb into the chair on my right before he got in the one to my left. I sat down in my little chair and because they were sitting above me, I felt like I was in front of a king and queen.

Mrs. Stanford spoke first. "J, I'm Erica Stanford. It's really nice to get to talk to you today. I think what your grandfather is doing is just wonderful and I'm honored to be a part of it."

"And I'm Don," Mr. Stanford said. "We've known your uncle Jeff a long time. He coached our son, Paul, in tee ball and the two of them remained close."

The tear finally fell from Mrs. Stanford's right eye. Swap handed her a rolled up wad of toilet paper.

"Sorry, we don't normally have tissues at the store," he said.

She laughed and wiped her cheek. "This is perfect, thank you."

"J," she continued, "we lost Paul just three days after he turned nineteen, October 13, 2008. He was a sophomore in college at the time."

Now I understood her emotions.

"Paul was a tall boy, just like his father, and he loved sports. It didn't matter what the season, Paul was on some team somewhere. As a child he was all boy, climbing trees, getting dirty, breaking things."

"We had that in common too," Mr. Stanford said, smiling.

DECISIONS

"That's the truth. I never let Don do any work around the house because whatever got broken ended up being the least of our problems when he was finished."

"It's not that bad, honey." As he was leaning over to talk to her, the arm rest on his chair cracked. He lifted his arm to look at the damage, "Well, maybe it is." Everyone laughed. Jeff grabbed a towel and some duct tape. He folded the towel a few times, set it on the cracked arm rest, and wrapped the silver tape around them both.

"Yet another use for duct tape," he said.

"Why don't you continue, honey. I'll try not to break anything else," Mr. Stanford said.

"J, I could never understand it. Give my husband a scalpel and put him in an operating room, and he was magnificent, the best surgeon around. People came from all over to see him. But give him a hammer or screwdriver and forget about it. Paul, however, could fix anything. He started teaching himself how to work on cars when he was fourteen, and in a couple years we didn't have to go to mechanics anymore. We actually just sold the old Land Cruiser he fixed up."

Mr. Stanford took over. "It was a 1963 Toyota J40 Land Cruiser; he found it rusting away in a parts yard. He liked it the moment he saw it and he became obsessed. He was only sixteen at the time, but he worked out a deal with the guy who ran the salvage yard to exchange labor for the old beast and whatever parts he could find to fix it up. He actually called it 'The Beast.' Over the next couple years, he replaced every mechanical piece of that vehicle, got the seats re-covered, and

SEASONS

replaced any part of the body that had rust. We have a picture of it when he got it all working and it had four different paint colors. He was proud of that thing. As a graduation gift, we gave him the money to put new tires on it and have it painted. He got top of the line tires, but he didn't want the glossy paint that's on cars you see today, so he had them paint it with the original mustard yellow on the bottom half and ivory white on the top. It's been in our garage since he died. I'd drive it around every once in a while to keep it from locking up and it was always a fun reminder of Paul. But, like Erica said, we decided to sell it recently. We felt like Paul would have wanted someone to enjoy it, and leaving it cooped up in our garage just didn't seem right anymore."

"I bet you're right," Jeff said. "He would have wanted someone to be driving The Beast."

Mrs. Stanford spoke, "He would have. That's just the kind of kid he was. He really cared about people and seemed to enjoy doing things for others. But everything changed when he went off to college. Things were fine for the first month or so, but before Thanksgiving he started acting different."

"What was he doing?" I asked.

"Small things at first," she said. "Forgetting to call when he said he would, being short when we did get to speak, letting his grades slip. Initially, we figured it was what all kids went through when they went off to college. We thought he was just discovering his new boundaries and trying to be more independent. It was too late before we knew the truth."

DECISIONS

I was as curious as ever, but I didn't have the nerve to ask them directly what happened. Mr. Stanford picked up the story. "J, he never got along with the roommate the college assigned him, so he set out to meet people in other places. He found a group of guys who also liked cars, but unfortunately they also liked a bunch of questionable stuff too."

"Like what?"

"Well, they did typical immature things like staying up late, skipping classes and drinking, but they didn't know where to stop. They experimented with whatever drug they could get their hands on. I don't think any of them had any specific addiction; they were just willing to try anything. They were reckless. We didn't know about it when it happened, but one of the guys Paul seemed to like got shot by one of the other guys. They were strung out on something and started to play a hunting game. Paul's buddy was pretending to be a deer and the other guy thought the gun was empty. It was just stupid. Thankfully, his leg took the brunt of it and he just ended up spending a long time in the hospital."

"Sorry to interrupt, but how did you learn all this after the fact?" I asked.

"He had opened a new Facebook account, using a nickname, and it was still open on his laptop when we went to clean out his room," Mr. Stanford said.

"It was both horrible and helpful." Mrs. Stanford wiped her cheeks with the toilet paper. "I hated that he had this secret life, and reading through the history of his messages was so hard. He was really not himself. But from it, we found out what happened and traced his story back to where it began. It was nice to have some answers even though we didn't like them."

"J," Swap said, "the Stanfords have actually put together a great talk they give on college campuses using Paul's story and screenshots from that Facebook account. I've heard it's very powerful."

"Oh, I'm sure. People don't seem to hold back on Facebook."

"Well, he did, at least to us," Mrs. Stanford said. "His 'Paul Stanford' page was as clean cut as it always was. It was the secret page where he had no boundaries. He was literally leading a double life."

"What did you find out happened to Paul?"

"Paul died from a severely bad reaction to some drug experiment. The toxicology report revealed traces of something called ethylene glycol."

"Ethylene glycol?"

"It's an ingredient in antifreeze," Mr. Stanford said. "One of their dangerous hobbies was mixing random household products in their alcohol. His blood alcohol was quite high, but it was the ethylene glycol that killed him. If someone had known what happened, there was a chance he could have been treated, but there wasn't a sober person in the room. They must have assumed he just passed out, when in truth, he experienced organ failure, slipped into a coma, and died sometime in the night. When his," he held up his hands, bending his fingers to make quotation marks, "'friends' found

DECISIONS

him the next morning, they drove him to the emergency room and literally left him on the sidewalk out front."

"That's horrible," I said.

Mrs. Stanford's eyes focused on mine. "It was horrible. But we've come to realize the boys he was hanging out with were probably just like Paul at one point. No doubt, they had parents who felt just like we did. At first we were profoundly angry, even to the point of hate. But we realized these guys represented something in Paul, and our hearts started to change for them. We began to reach out to them, to try to help. They are the reason we've started telling Paul's story. We don't want them to end up in the same situation. We don't want any other families to get the call we received."

"It's not their fault Paul's gone," Mr. Stanford said. "Paul made his own choices. Their choices certainly didn't help the matter, but if Paul had used a little wisdom he would be here today."

"You're better people than I am," Jeff said. "I'm still mad at them." Jeff had been so quiet I'd forgotten we were talking about someone he cared about, too. His jaw was set and his eyes were red with tears as he spoke. "If they wouldn't have been so stupid, Paul would have never had a drink spiked with antifreeze!"

Mrs. Stanford looked at him, tears in her eyes too. "You're right, Jeff. But Paul didn't have to be at that party and he didn't have to have a drink at all. He knew what they did to their alcohol. He might have been foolish, but he wasn't ignorant."

SEASONS

"I know," Jeff said, "but still …" His voice trailed off. Swap got Jeff some water and placed a hand on his shoulder as he drank.

"J," Mr. Stanford said, "have you ever heard the proverb 'He who walks with the wise grows wise, but a companion of fools suffers harm'?"

"Actually, one of the other guys brought it up at lunch today."

"That idea frames the talk we give at the colleges. We focus on the wise when we speak to them, because knowing what the wise look like is the best way to avoid the fools. So the first thing we try to teach them is how to identify the wise."

"What do you tell them?"

"It's tough. Wisdom is knowing the right thing do to when the answer isn't obvious. For instance, it doesn't require a lot of wisdom to know stealing a car is wrong. That's common sense stuff. Wisdom anticipates consequences, really thinks about cause and effect, and considers how a given decision will affect other people. It's self-benefitting but not self-serving. However, you can't look at a person and know they have wisdom. We give the students some ideas for how to narrow the field. We tell them to look for people who respect authority, who don't repeat foolish mistakes, who are responsible, and who have some sort of code or values they live by. At least this way, as they determine if someone is truly wise, they aren't getting into foolish trouble along the way."

"It seems like it would be easy to know who's wise and who's foolish. What am I missing?"

DECISIONS

"It's not as simple as you think because you don't have much to go on when you first meet somebody. You might know they show up to class on time and finish their assignments on time, but that really doesn't tell you if they're wise. Really applying this idea will involve meeting people, and then once you've gotten to know them a little, possibly cutting ties. That's not easy, especially when you're eager to make new friends."

"Oh so, you're saying Paul should have distanced himself from those guys once he realized what they were about."

"Yes."

"But since he was eager to have friends, he might have used poor judgment and got himself into a bad situation."

"That's how it appears. Have you ever known a girl who started dating a guy, and the guy was a jerk, but no matter what her friends said to her she wouldn't break up with him?"

"Are you kidding? All the time."

"Then you've seen what I'm talking about. She's gotten emotionally connected to the guy and her affection has clouded her judgment. She'll overlook foolishness. She'll justify his carelessness or even his cruelty. And normally, there were red flags early in the relationship that she missed or ignored. To identify the wise you have to be paying close attention and you have to be willing to get out of unhealthy relationships quickly, even if it means losing your only friends."

"I guess that could be hard, but hopefully the guys on the team are good guys and I won't have to worry about this."

SEASONS

"There are over one hundred guys on a college football team, J," Swap said. "Some will be wise, some will be fools; it's still up to you to choose wisely who you hang out with."

"And the cool thing is," Mr. Stanford said, "as you patiently choose wise friends, other people who are doing the same will find you because you are showing yourself to be wise. Either way you go, wise or foolish, it can snowball."

"Okay, but let's say I've found a couple good friends. Then what?"

"That's the next part of the process. Once you've identified the wise, you must walk with them," Mr. Stanford said.

His wife took over from there, "This is harder than it sounds."

"I was gonna say, isn't walking with them obvious once you know who they are?"

"You've got to define 'walk.' We're not talking about just playing XBox together or being at practice at the same time. Our idea of walk involves having the commitment to learn from each other and the courage to teach each other if need be. Beyond that, it may require you to walk past easy relationships with your roommate, guys in your dorm, or people in your class, in order to invest your time in the healthy relationship. It's the difference between being carried by the current and swimming upstream; both require a decision, but one – walking with the wise – requires much more effort."

"Ultimately," Mr. Stanford said, "this whole process is about decision making. People seem to be willing to give up better options in order to have the convenient ones. For example, grabbing a fast food hamburger is convenient, but not as

DECISIONS

healthy as going home and having a proper meal. We've seen that people, young people especially, are content being carried along by the convenient current in culture. Just look at alcohol consumption when kids get to college. Many just start drinking heavily almost as a rite of passage, without ever really thinking about the consequences. And remember, people who are wise consider consequences and think about how their choices will affect other people."

"I was telling the guys earlier how there were some guys on my team who were slackers and how much it bothered me when they hurt the team. It sounds kind of like what you're talking about."

"That's a great example, J," Mrs. Stanford said. "The only difference is we're talking about living life, whereas you were just playing games. If you're slack with your workouts, the consequence might be a lack of playing time. But if you're slack with your decision making in the real world, it could, well, just look at what happened to Paul."

Everyone was quiet for a moment. I was trying to let what the Stanfords were telling me sink in. Jeff was still a little emotional, but my grandpa was standing with him. Finally, Mr. Stanford picked the conversation back up.

"You've got to learn from the people in your life, J, both the wise and the fools. Part of walking with the wise includes learning and developing from the example of those with whom you walk. But you can, and should, be learning from those who are older as well. Identifying the wise still applies though; just being older doesn't make someone wiser. But as you identify men and women of wisdom, learn from them. Some have written great books. Read them and see what you can apply in your life. Observe your coaches off the football field and see how they're living life. Learn what you can. Almost every decision you'll ever make was made previously by someone else, and a wise man seeks to learn from the example of others. We'd like to think our conversation today, and Paul's life, would lead you to walk away from similar circumstances, but some people will hear this and still make foolish choices. They're convinced it won't happen to them and they refuse to learn from the example of others."

"And the powerful thing about all this," Mrs. Stanford said, "is as you walk and learn from the wise, you grow in wisdom yourself. I would never encourage you to walk alone, but as you become wiser you become a person worth following; a person others will seek out and want to learn from."

"Like you said, 'he who walks with the wise grows wise,'" I said.

Swap patted Jeff on the shoulder and walked over to the Stanfords. "Don, Erica, I can't tell you how grateful I am that you came down here to talk to J. I can't imagine how hard it's been to live without Paul, but I know you honor him as you tell his story."

"Thanks, Swap," Mr. Stanford said. "But it truly was our pleasure. You're doing a good thing here and we were glad to be a part of it."

Jeff walked over and gave each of them a hug. I stood as well, off to the side. Mrs. Stanford hugged him the longest, a

DECISIONS

mother's embrace. I wondered if it was as much for her as it was for Jeff.

Mr. Stanford walked toward me and shook my hand. "J, you've got wise people around you already. Listen to them. Learn from them. You're going to do great at college. I'll be looking for you on TV in the fall."

"I doubt I get on the field much this fall, but maybe next year."

"Then next year it is. I'm sure Jeff will keep me up to date until then." He put his hand on his wife's back and she let go of Jeff. Then she turned to me and stood next to Mr. Stanford, his left arm around her shoulder.

"Just remember, your choices have consequences far beyond just you. There are people at home who love you and want the best for you. If you find yourself in a tight spot, remember them. Remember your mother. Remember Swap and Jeff. Remember me and our talk today if you must, but find something to hang on to and let it pull you out of bad places."

"I will, Mrs. Stanford. I promise."

The couple walked out the door, Mr. Stanford stepping aside to let her exit first. Once they were gone, Swap said, "What a story."

"It really was," I said.

"Well, I hope you'll take it to heart, J," Jeff said, "especially the part about thinking about how your choices affect others, because they do." He said no more, but he walked to the front window and flipped the sign back to "open." I went to let

SEASONS

Slobber out of the bathroom, but when I opened the door he was snoring, so I just left it open and went back to the shop. Lazy old dog.

DISCUSSION QUESTIONS

1. A big theme in this chapter is how people influence one another. Just talk about how you've seen this at work in your life or in the lives of people around you.

2. The Stanfords said the foundation of their message to college students in the proverb, "He who walks with the wise grows wise, but a companion of fools suffers harm." What do you think about that idea? Have you ever experienced either scenario, growing in wisdom or suffering harm, as a result of the people you were spending time with?

3. Mr. Stanford said, "You have to be willing to get out of unhealthy relationships quickly, even if it means losing your only friends." Would you say that's accurate, a bit dramatic, or nonsense? Why? Have you ever had to walk away from an unhealthy relationship? How did you feel in the weeks preceding and the weeks after the relationship ended?

4. Mr. Stanford said, "You've got to learn from the people in your life, both the wise and the fools." How do you think you do that? What are some of the benefits from learning from fools?

SEASONS

5. What do you think about Mrs. Stanford's statement, "I would never encourage you to walk alone, but as you become wiser you become a person worth following; a person others will seek out and want to learn from."

– chapter ten –

CAN YOU LEAD YOU?

*Leaders are molded from the highest character
and are generally the hardest workers on the team.
They're the first to come to practice and the last ones to leave.
During practice, they lead by example with
their mouths closed, concentrating hard.
They understand the team's goals so they know
what has to be done. They realize that practice is precious
preparation time for the real thing – the match.*
– DAN GABLE, sixteen-time NCAA champion wrestling coach

*... I've never been captain in 16 years in the NHL.
But that didn't stop me from being a leader in my own way.*
– GUY LAFLEUR, five-time Stanley Cup winner

SEASONS

NOT MUCH TALKING HAPPENED between visitors this time. Jeff and I both flipped through magazines, while my grandpa tried to see if he could fix the arm rest on the chair Mr. Stanford broke. I went to use the bathroom and when I walked back out, the man I assumed to be my next mentor was already sitting by my grandfather. He was a shorter, thinner version of Tyler Perry; I had to look twice to be sure it wasn't him. The man stood when I walked over and introduced himself, "J, I'm John Stanley." He looked me dead in the eye and gave me a firm handshake. "I've known your grandfather for a long time and I'm excited to talk with you today." He was dressed like my principal but without the radio attached to his belt — simple brown leather shoes, tan pants, and a shirt striped with several of different shades of green.

"It's nice to meet you, sir."

"From what I hear," he nodded over his shoulder toward my grandpa, "the pleasure's all mine. Swap says you're quite the ball player."

"I can hold my own."

"Oh, so now you're going to be humble?" Jeff never took his eyes off his magazine.

"I'm humble, Jeff. Just not around you because you make me look so good." He kept reading.

"J, I'm the CEO of a little not-for-profit group and I do consulting work for other non-profits. Swap asked me to speak with you about leadership." He handed me a business card. It said, "Lead One," in gold block letters, and then just

LEADERSHIP

beneath that was his name in smaller black script. I flipped it over and found all kinds of contact information. I stuck it in my pocket.

"I've always wondered what exactly a consultant does."

"Simply put, I get to give other people advice on how to run their businesses. Sometimes, having an outsider's perspective can help get you out of a rut."

"What kind of stuff do you do exactly?"

"I'll look over their budgets and look for areas where they can be more efficient. I'll interview employees to see if they feel productive and understand the company's purpose. I talk with some of the company's clients to get their perspective. Once I've done my research, I talk with the leader and give them my advice."

"And they pay you for that?"

"Believe it or not, guys like me in the profit world make big money doing this work."

"Why aren't you in the profit world making big money?"

"Well, because making big money was never my purpose. Don't get me wrong, I want to make a living and provide for my family, but I never felt like I needed big money to do that. I want to help companies that do work I believe in, do their work better. I feel like I'm making a difference, you know?"

"I get that, but I'd like to make the big money *and* help people."

"I hope you do. I work with big money people all the time; their contributions make many of the companies I work for run. Actually, most non-profits are dependant on the support of generous, big money people. We all have a part to play."

"Maybe one day I can be one of those generous people helping your companies."

"Maybe. But let me ask you something." He was smiling, but very serious. "Are you generous now?"

"I don't have any money. How could I be generous?"

"You don't measure generosity by how much someone gives; you measure generosity by how much someone keeps."

"Then I'm definitely not generous, because I spend what little I get. But that will change when I have more."

"You think so?"

"Of course. If I have more money, I'll be able to give more money."

"You're right. You'll be able to give more money. But generosity isn't measured by how much you give, remember?"

"I remember, but I'm not sure I agree with your definition anymore."

"And when you understand why you changed your mind, you'll be ready to lead."

"What does this have to do with being a leader?"

"Who said anything about being a leader?" He had that serious smile again.

I looked at my grandpa for some help, but he had the same smile as Mr. Stanley. I slowly answered, "You said something about being a leader."

"No, I didn't. I said you'll be ready to lead. I never said anything about being a leader."

LEADERSHIP

"That's the same thing."

"And when you understand how they're different, you'll be ready to lead."

He grinned again, and this time I found it a little annoying. Beginning to feel defensive, I said, "Apparently I'm not ready to lead, because I've got no idea what you're talking about, but my coach always said I was a leader."

"And I'm sure you were a good one. Assuming Swap's boasting was at least partly true, you were the best player on your team. Oftentimes, great players have leadership thrust upon them, especially in high school. The team's business is making plays and because you make so many of them, you become the leader. But being a great runner or tackler doesn't automatically mean you have the capacity to lead well. Your talent gives you the opportunity to lead; your character determines if you do it well. Let me ask you a question, did you desire to be a leader or a great player?"

"I wanted to be a great player."

"What were some of the things you had to do to become a great player?"

"I don't know, the regular stuff I guess: work hard at practice, lift weights, watch film, stay out of trouble. Stuff like that."

"That's regular stuff?"

"Sure."

"So why wasn't everyone on your team great?"

"Some of the guys just weren't good enough. They played hard, but sometimes one hundred thirty pounds just can't play hard enough."

SEASONS

"Sure, talent and size go a long way in making a great player, but most things you'll do don't place as much emphasis on size and speed. What about the guys who could run and were big enough, were they all great?"

"No, I guess not."

"Why?"

"They didn't work as hard as they could have."

"So what you did wasn't regular stuff. The regular guys didn't work hard. The regular guys made excuses. The regular guys got in trouble. Special guys, guys like you, did just the opposite. J, you did the special stuff and that's why you were a good leader."

"Okay, but didn't we already establish that?"

"No. You said your coach called you a leader, but you didn't know why."

"I knew why. It's what you said: I made the most plays."

"Right, because you made plays, your coach gave you the title of leader. But what allowed you to make those plays?"

"Practice and stuff."

"Exactly. You did the special stuff because you wanted to be a great player and when you were given the chance to lead, you just had to keep doing what you were already doing. That's the secret."

"What's the secret?"

"The secret to being a great leader is to stop trying to be a leader."

"I'm afraid I don't follow."

"Do you know who Vince Lombardi is?"

LEADERSHIP

"Yep, he coached the Packers and they named the Super Bowl trophy after him."

"Well, he said, 'Leaders aren't born, they are made. And they are made just like anything else, through hard work. And that's the price we'll have to pay to achieve that goal, or any goal.' Do you think Lombardi had his teams spending practice time working on leadership?"

"I doubt it. They were probably practicing football."

"That's exactly what they were doing, playing football. Leading well is the result of living well, and on the football field living well is about hard work, sweat, knowing your plays, and so on If you do those things, you will lead well. However, if you just seek to be a leader, you'll get it all messed up."

"So, Lombardi was just saying the leaders rose to the top because of how hard they worked."

"That's exactly what he was saying. Now he had some truly special leaders. Lombardi's quarterback, Bart Starr, for instance, had that unique mix of superior talent and a superior work ethic that produces legends. But the talent part isn't in your hands, so you can't worry about being a legend. You focus on the other part: the character and work ethic; and legend or not, you will be able to lead well."

"So you're telling me I shouldn't worry about being a leader?"

"Correct. Don't worry so much about being a leader; instead worry about being prepared to lead well. Leader is a title, leading well is an attitude."

"It's simple really. I'd just really never thought about it like that."

SEASONS

"You may not have thought about it, but you already knew it."

"Okay, but what does it have to do with being generous?"

"Everything."

"Care to explain?"

"I once heard a guy say, 'A leader of one can be the leader of many, but if you can't lead one, you can't lead any.' What do you think that means?"

"That I've got to take care of myself before I worry about taking care of everybody else?"

"Yeah, that's basically it, although I wouldn't use those words exactly. The principle is this: learn to control yourself before you worry about controlling others. And you learn to control yourself right now, not later."

"Okay, but how does this relate to being generous?"

"You said you would be generous later, when you had more money."

"Right."

"Well, you don't just flip a switch and become generous anymore than you just flip a switch and become a hard worker. You said yourself; there were plenty of guys with ability who were content being regular."

"But what does skill have to do with money?"

"It's not so much about having skill and money; it's about how you manage them. If you want to be a generous person when you have big money, start being a generous person now. Lead one."

"But how can I be generous if I don't have a lot of money?"

LEADERSHIP

"Remember it's not what you give, but what you keep. We've confused generosity with giving a lot of money. But there are people in this world who write huge checks to create a façade of generosity when in truth their seemingly huge check is insignificant when contrasted with their net worth. A person can give the appearance of being generous by writing a big check, but if that big check is small compared to what they keep, it's a front. You might not be able to write the big check today, but that shouldn't stop you from being generous."

"And you're saying if I'm generous now, I'll be generous later."

"It's just like taking the proper steps on the field. Your coach makes you practice them over and over to develop the habit. Then, when your talent blossoms, you have the necessary habits to be highly efficient. The truth is, you're developing habits now whether you realize it or not, but the question is, are they healthy ones? If your money habit is to keep everything, that habit will still be there when you have big money. However, if your habit is to be generous, that habit will be there when you have big money."

"That makes sense. But how does it connect to being a leader?"

"It doesn't. But it does connect to being able to lead well. The prideful man seeks followers where the humble man seeks to serve, and the humble man leads well. How you manage your money reveals a lot about your willingness to serve. When you do get money, how often do you think of how that money could serve someone else?"

SEASONS

"Almost never. What difference is a couple dollars going to make?"

"It depends on who you're giving it to. I bet you know plenty of people who don't have the same advantages you have. To them, something as simple as taking them to Taco Bell could be a real blessing. It isn't how much you give, but how much you keep. If you had ten bucks, and spent it taking you and a friend out for burritos, you would be developing a habit of keeping only half. That's huge! And that's generous by only giving five dollars. And that's leading well."

"I'm still not sure I see the connection."

"The desire to be rich will overwhelm the desire to be generous as sure as the desire to be a leader will overwhelm the desire to lead well."

"Say that again," I asked, closing my eyes to focus on the words.

"The desire to be rich will overwhelm the desire to be generous as sure as the desire to be a leader will overwhelm the desire to lead well. Seeking to be a leader is selfish like seeking to be rich is selfish. Often the two are connected. Most people who want to be leaders really just want to be rich and think being a leader is the trick to wealth. But seeking to lead well is selfless just as seeking to be generous is selfless. They are both attitudes of humility and sacrifice and those are the characteristics of one who leads well."

"That's cool."

"A man once said, 'Courage is not limited to the battlefield, or the Indianapolis 500, or bravely catching the thief in your

LEADERSHIP

house. The real tests of courage are much quieter. They are the inner test, such as remaining faithful when nobody's looking, enduring pain when the room is empty or standing alone when you're misunderstood.'[1] When we think about leadership, we think of those battlefields, but leading well on the battlefield happens as the result of leading well when nobody's looking, when you're all alone, because leading others well begins with leading yourself well. Don't seek to be a leader, J. Seek to lead well and let the title of leader take care of itself."

"If I just keep my head down and do what I'm supposed to do, I'll become a good leader?"

"No. You will already be a good leader."

"But how can you say I would already be a good leader if there was no one following me?"

"For two reasons: one, because in some sort of metaphysical way you would be following yourself; and two, because great leaders don't need followers."

"Great leaders don't need followers? Then what are we talking about?"

"We're talking about greatness."

"We're not talking about leadership?"

"No. The idea of leadership is a stumbling block: it's fools gold. Forget leadership and just be a leader. Greatness shows up in the little things, the anonymous things. Greatness is in your attitude. As you pursue true greatness, you're leading one. As you lead one, you prepare yourself to lead many, and you might just turn around and find you have followers."

SEASONS

"I thought a great leader doesn't need followers?"

"They don't. A great leader needs a personal challenge, a calling, or a standard to live up to. It doesn't matter if he's leading one or leading millions because his greatness is developed in the moments when no one's watching anyway."

"So when do followers come in?"

Mr. Stanley paused for a moment, his mind searching for what he wanted to say. Then his eyes lit up and with a grin he said, "Do you like chocolate chip cookies?"

"Sure."

"I'm not talking about the bag cookies from a store." He closed his eyes, tilted his head toward the ceiling, and took a deep breath. He exhaled with a grin. "I'm talking about fresh out of the oven cookies. The ones that are so soft you have to pick them up with two hands, so warm they cover your fingers with still melting chocolate. Is that the kind you like?"

"Doesn't everybody?"

"Have you ever been doing your homework or something and been surprised by the sweet smell of cookies in the oven?"

"Many times. My mom makes sinful chocolate chip and oatmeal cookies, and when they're baking, the aroma will stop you dead in your tracks and drag you to the kitchen."

"That's where the followers come in."

His change of subject ruined my daydream. "You want me to bake cookies?"

He laughed. "The point is, you were drawn to the kitchen because you noticed what your mom was doing, and you

LEADERSHIP

liked it. The doing came first. And because what she was doing was so great, followers were inevitable. If she was just standing around the kitchen hoping people would come, she would have waited a long time."

"But eventually people would have come because they were hungry."

"You're right. Let's say that hungry person was you. Your grumbling stomach forces you to stop what you're doing and you find your mom in the kitchen. And let's say you ask your mom to make you something to eat. Now listen to me, J, don't miss this. In the fresh baked cookie scenario you were drawn by what she did, but in the second example you were drawn by what you needed, and she just happened to be there. In that second example, the kitchen could have been empty, or we could replace your mom with a juggler in clown's makeup and you still would have been there. Believe me, there are plenty of clowns sitting in positions of leadership, convinced they're the reason people come, but in reality they're just in the way. If you have followers, you want them to be there because you make great cookies, not just because you happen to be the one in the kitchen."

"So, it's not that followers are bad, just that they don't tell the whole story?"

"You got it. A person who craves followers will fight others to impress them, but a person who craves greatness will fight himself and attract them. Both may have followers, but only one is worth following. Which one will you be?"

"I'll be the person who chases greatness."

SEASONS

"It's not a tomorrow thing, J. You're either pursuing greatness or you're not. So which is it?"

"I am a person who's pursuing greatness."

"Then you're a leader of one, and that's where all history's great leaders began."

"Easy enough."

Mr. Stanley leaned forward in his chair. "No, it's not easy at all. Attracting followers or gaining titles is easy. To lead yourself is to have your greatest critic following you. And leading yourself is like trying to move a stubborn donkey sometimes. It's not easy to get out of bed when the alarm goes off. Shoot, it's not easy to set the alarm in the first place, but those leading themselves do it anyway. Other people will tell you how great you are, but the lazy person you're leading first will constantly complain and remind you of your failures. Leading a critical, lazy person is the farthest thing from 'easy enough,' and the sooner you accept that, the better."

"Then I'm up to the challenge. Bring that lazy, critical old fool on, and I'll whip him into shape."

Mr. Stanley smiled. "That's the spirit." He stood from his chair, walked over to me, and placed his hand on my shoulder. "I believe it was Plato who said, 'For a man to conquer himself is the first and noblest of all victories.' If you make conquering yourself the first battle, you win every day. Greatness will be your reward."

"Then I'll consider my alarm clock the opening bell of a boxing round against myself, and I think it was Ivan Drago

LEADERSHIP

who said," and I spoke out in my best Russian accent, snarling my top lip, "'If he dies, he dies.'"

He laughed. "And if you match the heart of Rocky with the ability of Drago, you'll be unstoppable."

He said goodbye to Jeff and my grandpa and left the store. I sat in my chair imagining *Rocky* scenes and pumped my fists like the Italian Stallion in one of his training montages. Jeff laughed at me, shaking his head. So I looked at him and said, "I pity the fool who shakes his head at me!"

"Um, J. That's a line from Mr. T, not Rocky," Jeff said.

"Well, Rocky or not, you know what I mean."

With a little extra enthusiasm, Jeff shook his head at me again, and I couldn't help but laugh.

[1] Charles Swindoll

DISCUSSION QUESTIONS

1. What do you think about John Stanley's statement, "You don't measure generosity by how much someone gives; you measure generosity by how much someone keeps"?

2. Talk about the following statements: "The secret to being a great leader is to stop trying to be a leader" and "Leading well is the result of living well."

3. Mr. Stanley stressed the importance of practicing habits now that we hope to have in the future, and he went so far as to say the habits you have now will be the ones you have later, even if they are unhealthy ones. How does that idea affect you? Here's an example: Many people hope to be a good husband or good wife one day, but are you practicing healthy husband or wife habits within your relationships now? Assuming you were married, would your current behavior honor your spouse and your vows? What do you think?

4. What do you think about the idea that a great leader doesn't need followers, a great leader just needs a personal challenge? What are some of the dangers of seeking followers? What are some challenges you can give yourself to start being a leader of one?

LEADERSHIP

5. "A person who craves followers will fight others to impress them, but a person who craves greatness will fight himself and attract them." Try to state that idea in your own words. What do you think it means? Have you ever seen someone fight others to impress potential followers?

– chapter eleven –

OPPORTUNITIES

WILL YOU BE READY?

*Setting a goal is not the main thing.
It is deciding how you will go about achieving it
and staying with that plan.*
– TOM LANDRY, 1990 Pro Football Hall of Fame inductee

*If you're going to lead, you need to make goals.
And those goals can't come from the top down,
they've got to come from the people
who are responsible for achieving them.
Your job is to help them get there,
and remind them every day what their goals are,
and what they have to do to make their dreams come true.*
– BO SCHEMBECHLER,
1993 College Football Hall of Fame inductee

SEASONS

I TOOK MY PHONE OUT OF MY POCKET to see what time it was and saw I had missed a text from my mom, "*How's it going?*" She'd sent it at around lunch time, and since it was after two o'clock, I figured I should at least touch base. "*Fine.*" She must have been staring at her phone waiting for me to respond, because her reply arrived in seconds. "*That's good. Don't forget the milk. Love you this much...*" She wrote that a lot. It was from a book she read to me as a little kid. The story was about a rabbit and his mom and they took turns saying how much they loved each other. I replied, "*Love you right up to the moon*", and put my phone back in my pocket.

Jeff reminded me Mr. T actually played Rocky's opponent, Clubber Lang, in *Rocky III*, which got us into a debate about who was the best villain in the *Rocky* series. Jeff tried to get philosophical and convince me Rocky was his own greatest enemy, but we eventually agreed Drago was the best. We were in an exchange of quotes from the movies when a man walked in holding hands with a little boy in a *Star Wars* T-shirt. The kid climbed into Swap's chair and the man sat across from him, a couple chairs to my left.

"Hey, guys. Need the regular, Ben?" my grandpa asked the boy.

"Yes. I need all of my hairs cut, but not too short or my mom won't let my dad eat dinner."

The man in the chair smirked and shook his head, "He speaks the truth."

Swap laughed as he wrapped the cloth around his tiny customer. The boy kicked the cloth playfully while my grandpa

OPPORTUNITIES

started to work. A few minutes later, another man showed up. He was a big guy, broad shoulders and at least six foot three. He didn't seem interested in a hair cut so I figured he was there to talk to me.

"Hey, Tom," Swap said.

"Hey, Swap. Where should I sit?"

"Anywhere you want."

"He can't sit here," the boy said.

"Please excuse me," my grandpa said, playfully bowing to the boy. "Sit anywhere except here."

The man sat down next to me. "Judging between the two of you," he said, nodding toward Swap's customer, "I'm gonna guess you're J. Am I right?"

"Yes, sir."

"Well, it's nice to finally meet you." He then looked past me to Jeff, "Must be quite an article you're reading over there."

I turned to look and saw that somehow, in a matter of seconds, Jeff had fallen asleep with the magazine in his lap and his phone on the page. Swap said, "I swear the man is narcoleptic. He does this all the time. One minute you're having a conversation and the next he's snoring. I've never seen anything like it."

Never one to miss an opportunity, I gently picked up his phone, set it to silent, and hid it in the stack of magazines. Then I went to the bathroom and picked up Slobber. When Swap saw me carrying the dog, he rolled his eyes and went back to his task. The boy was wide-eyed, eager to see what was about to happen. I walked up to Jeff's chair and held

SEASONS

Slobber's face as close to Jeff's face as I could, letting the dog breathe right at his nose. Jeff wrinkled his nose a few times before Slobber started licking his face like it was brisket. It took a few seconds for Jeff to realize what was happening, but once he did, he jumped and flung the magazine, yelping just a little bit. "J, I swear, if your grandfather wasn't my boss, I'd take you out back right now." He wiped his sleeve over his mouth and spit into his arm, "That's just gross." He started for the bathroom, "Hey, Tom. Thanks for the help."

Tom laughed, "I had nothing to do with it."

I put the dog down and he chased Jeff into the bathroom. Swap had to stop cutting the boy's hair because the little *Star Wars* fan was laughing too hard to sit still.

"Don't you go getting any ideas, Ben," his dad said. I don't think the boy heard him.

"Sorry, Tom, it was something that had to be done," I said.

"No apology necessary, you have to do what you have to do."

"J, this is Thomas Cothran. He was a linebacker at State a couple years before you."

"A couple decades maybe," the man said. His long sleeve, Winter Park, Colorado T-shirt was tucked neatly into his jeans. He had on a pair of nice black and brown tennis shoes with thick, dark socks that matched his shirt. A pair of glasses hung from his shirt collar. "Swap asked me to come introduce myself and tell you some of my story. He thinks we might have a little in common."

"Well, football's one of them. What years were you at State?"

OPPORTUNITIES

"I played from '77 to '81. Well, I was on the team all those years. I only played in '80 and '81."

"You were on one of the championship teams then?"

"Yep. We won the conference my senior year."

"And you were a linebacker?"

"Yeah. I started on the outside but wasn't quite quick enough, so they moved me to the middle. I was all-conference as a senior but nowhere near good enough for the next level."

"I mean this as a compliment, but you don't really have the classic linebacker look." He looked far too kind and lighthearted to be a middle linebacker.

"My college self might have been offended by that, but the man you see today takes it as a compliment, I think."

"I mean, you just don't look mean."

"You mean, he's not mean? Well, that's mean, if you know what I mean," Swap said, smiling, but still moving his scissors around the boy's ear.

"Would it be mean if the next time you fell asleep I let you get up close and personal with Slobber," I asked, smiling.

"You do that and I'll shave your hair and eyebrows while you sleep. Never mess with a barber, son."

"Hopefully I don't get on either of your bad sides. You guys are serious."

"More like clowns," Jeff said, walking back into the room. "You can't take 'em anywhere. J's a kid, so I give him a pass for being part of 'generation nonsense,' but Swap doesn't have that excuse. He should know better." He picked his magazine off the floor and sat down to find where he was reading. "Have you guys seen my phone?"

"You can't find it?" I asked. "Maybe your wife put it with her keys."

"Oh, you've got jokes now too? Where's my phone?"

"I'm sorry, but I'm in the middle of an important conversation. What were you saying, Tom?"

"I was about to tell you a little bit of my story."

"That's right. Please excuse Jeff. He never knows when to be serious."

"Well, I wasn't as decorated as you were in high school. I was good, but there weren't many schools interested. Remember, I was a little too small to play inside in college, but a little too slow to play outside. My father went to State and my brother was already a sophomore there so that's where I went. And since I was there, I decided to walk on. I made the team and lived at the bottom of the depth chart for the next couple years."

"That had to be frustrating, after being a starter in high school."

"It was, but there were hardly any players in my class getting much playing time. We weren't as developed as young kids are today, so most of us spent the first couple years bulking up and adjusting to the speed of college ball. I wasn't too discouraged, but I wasn't going to let playing time discourage me anyway."

"Why? I mean, why wouldn't you want playing time?"

OPPORTUNITIES

"I didn't say I didn't want playing time. I wanted to play so bad it hurt. I said I wouldn't let a lack of playing time discourage me. I had no control over how much playing time I got. That's up to the coaches, so I just focused on what was up to me. In other words, I would never demand an opportunity, but I would be ready when my opportunity came."

"But two years? I don't know if I can be that patient."

"You don't have to be patient. I wasn't."

"You said you didn't play for two years and you didn't demand an opportunity. That's patience."

"No. That's not letting things outside of my control bother me. I wasn't patient at all. I set goals and worked like mad to attain them. I wasn't about to wait for something like playing time to start going after my goals."

"If you weren't on the field, how could you achieve any goals? You're not breaking any records on the bench."

"We apparently have different goals. Mine had nothing to do with statistics or records. Those are secondary, and they come and go. My goals had more to do with who I wanted to become as a person. I saw football as an opportunity to improve myself and my goals reflected that. Reaching my goals didn't depend on me getting playing time."

"So what kind of goals did you set?"

"I figured I needed to be ready for my opportunity when it came, but I didn't limit my potential opportunities to the football field. I focused on three things: having the best attitude possible, working harder each day than I had before, and being absolutely dependable, no excuses. Attitude, work ethic, and dependability transcend the field, so I set out to become excellent in each area."

"That's nice, but if you really wanted to play you would have to get better at football."

"And I did. And I got stronger. And I got faster. I tried to see each day as an opportunity, and hoped I'd get another opportunity the next day. I worked out vigorously, practiced with passionate intensity, and tried to implement everything a coach told me. As I focused on those three things, I became better at football, and readied myself for my eventual opportunity."

"You did get a chance to play then?"

"Sure did. I started for two years."

"How did you get your opportunity?"

"I didn't will it to be, that's for sure. I guess you could say I worked my way up to second string. The coached trusted me and liked me. And when I got on the practice field I could hold my own. But the guy in front of me was scary good. He had that nasty linebacker look you said I lack. But the problem was he was all talent and ability with no control or fundamentals. He was good enough to make plays on sheer talent, but he was undisciplined off the field. That's what led to my opportunity."

"How so?"

"Early on in two-a-days in 1980, the coaches were riding him pretty hard. I sincerely believe they thought he had a future in the NFL if he would focus, and they decided to try to get him to do just that. They were all over him. Even when

OPPORTUNITIES

he made plays they would jump him for his poor technique. It drove him crazy. He didn't like criticism."

"I don't either. Who does?"

"Criticism's part of the game, just like getting your head knocked or your foot stomped. Your coaches will criticize you every single day: it's what coaches do. Every day, they are trying to make you better than you were the day before, so they have to criticize something."

"Sure, but it still isn't fun."

"It isn't supposed to be fun. But is icing your body after a game fun? Are running dozens of sprints after an August practice fun? Do you enjoy repeating the same play over and over again? There is very little that's truly fun about the game of football. What we like is being on a team and fighting through stuff together, having people cheer for us, and winning games. And we know all that stuff that's no fun will provide the things we want. And that's a perfect metaphor for life."

"I guess I see your point."

"This guy didn't. He was convinced he was NFL ready and didn't need all their harassment. He started going out after practice to drink his frustrations away and one night got a D.U.I. on his way home. He ended up getting suspended, which gave me my first opportunity."

"Bad for him, but good for you I guess."

"It could have been good for him too if he would have learned from it. But he didn't. A few weeks after the first incident, he got another D.U.I. and was nailed for driving with a suspended license. And just like that, his career at State was over. Our coach would give you three chances, but this guy used his second and third in this one event. After he took himself out of the way, I started every game the rest of my career."

"That's cool."

"It was cool. I loved playing. But if my focus had been on playing time or statistics I might have quit long before my opportunity arrived. I knew guys that did."

"Really, you had teammates quit?"

"Sure, a couple of them. They couldn't hack it for whatever reason, and it's not for me to judge why they quit, but we'll never know if their opportunity was around the corner. They took themselves out of the game."

"And you think they quit because they were frustrated about playing time?"

"Like I said, it's not for me to judge, but I know a couple of the guys who left had convinced themselves they were the rightful starters."

"Do you think they could have played if they hadn't quit?"

"Without a doubt. They were very talented guys. They were just focused on the wrong thing. But now that I think about it, I'm not so sure anymore. Had they been given a shot, they might have responded the same way the guy in front of me did and failed. But we'll never know."

"Yeah, I guess not."

"Almost everyone has some kind of dream as a kid. We want to hit the World Series-winning, walk-off grand slam, or catch the game-winning Hail Mary, or win an Olympic gold. We think about what we want, but we never think

OPPORTUNITIES

about what we *don't* want and then the original goal leads us into temptation, if you will."

"What do you mean?"

"Think about all the people who've achieved some sort of professional success only to get busted for performance enhancing drugs, or street drugs, or gambling. You name it and somebody's been busted for it."

"Okay, but like you said, that happens all the time. I'm not going to be like that"

"Do you think when any of those guys were your age, talking about their futures, they told their friends that one day they hoped to get busted for drugs?"

"Of course not."

"Then what do you think happened?"

"I guess they got in a tight spot or something, I don't know."

"You're probably right. For whatever reason, they were presented with an opportunity that sounded good at the time and they took it, even though there was probably a time in their life they would have never considered it. That's how a lot of foolish things happen. A kid sees a pack of baseball cards he wants, he looks around the store and doesn't see anyone watching, so he sticks the pack in his pocket and walks out. Thirty seconds later he's getting arrested for shoplifting. I know because I've done it."

"You got arrested for stealing baseball cards?"

"Yep, but thankfully I was young and the situation burned a desire in me to avoid being in that place ever again."

"What are you saying I should do?"

SEASONS

"You have to have your goal, but you also have to know where the line is. What you want to avoid might be as simple as never being in the back of a police car, maybe it's as specific as I never want to become an alcoholic, or as intimate as never wanting to dishonor your family name. Just know where you don't want to go, and fight to avoid it."

"How do you do that?"

"Let's look at the alcoholic example. Let's imagine there has been alcoholism in your family and you decide it's not going to be true of you."

"Okay."

"So you need to think backwards from alcoholism and see how someone gets there. I promise you they didn't set a goal of alcoholism and worked to achieve it. One thing all alcoholics have in common is they all had a first drink, and maybe that's where your line would have to be. I know if I had a family history of alcoholism and I didn't want to become an alcoholic I would never take a sip. It would represent a step toward a place I didn't want to go, and the potential of becoming a major slide."

"Just say no. Right, I've heard that before."

"That's not what I'm saying. But I am saying you have to be ready for opportunities, both good and bad. If you want to be an NFL linebacker and you are presented with an opportunity to try HGH, what are you going to do?"

"I'm going to say no."

"Because of some silly add campaign from high school?"

"No, because it would be stupid."

OPPORTUNITIES

"Don't you think the guys that took it were aware of what it was and could do? They were just like you, driven to achieve a goal."

"Yeah, but obviously they had some character flaw."

"Maybe, but until you are in their situation it's a bit arrogant to think you know. However, I do think they were too focused on their achievement goal and lost sight of the line, or maybe never established a line in the first place. You can't afford to do that."

"So, I might say I want to be in the NFL, but I don't want to do anything illegal to get there?"

"Sure, that's a good start. Then you start to imagine potential scenarios and prepare yourself for them, just as you would for an upcoming opponent. What will you say and do if HGH shows up in the locker room one day? How will you respond if a booster offers to buy you dinner? Will you cheat on a test to stay on the field? Cheating may not land you in jail, but it's a step in jail's direction. It's like that first drink."

"So, I should imagine scenarios and start preparing a response."

"Exactly. Know what you want, and be ready when the opportunity arrives. But also know what you don't want and be ready for those opportunities as well."

"I get what you're saying, but it sounds like if I live like this, I'll miss out on all kinds of experiences, especially the ones you only get to do when you're young."

"Gummy Bears and a New York strip."

"What?"

SEASONS

"Gummy Bears and a New York strip."

"I heard you, but what does that mean?"

"That's what you're talking about."

"That's what *I'm* talking about?"

"Have you ever eaten a big handful of Gummy Bears?"

"Maybe as a little kid, but I really don't care for them."

"I have! I love Gummy bears!" The little boy almost cheered. His father grinned. Swap finished the boy's cut and began cleaning up.

"Then use your imagination. When you eat a big helping of Gummy Bears, a candy I actually enjoy, they kind of fill you up, and that full feeling can linger for longer than it does with other foods."

I looked at him and tried to hide my confusion, but wasn't successful, "Okay."

"There was a day, early in my marriage, when I was hungry after work and picked up a bag of Gummy Bears for my drive home. Of course, I ate the whole bag, happy as could be, probably listening to some mindless sports talk on the radio. I pulled into my driveway to head inside, but when I opened my car door I smelled them."

"Smelled what?"

"The New York strips. My wife had them on the grill about ready to serve. She had baked potatoes loaded and steaming in the kitchen, a caesar salad with real parmesan cheese chilled and waiting on the table, and even had made a loaf of bread from scratch which was warm and wrapped in a cloth on the table. It was a feast, and my absolute favorite meal."

OPPORTUNITIES

"And there was something wrong with that?" I asked.

"There was nothing wrong with the meal. But there was something wrong with the gross, full-of-Gummy Bears feeling in my stomach. There's an old saying, 'Hunger is the best spice,' and you might say a stomach full of Gummy Bears is the worst."

"Sorry for you, man."

"Oh, I ate my dinner, every bite. There's another old saying, 'Happy wife, happy life,' that's in play in this story too."

The three other men in the room nodded and enthusiastically agreed. Tom continued, "But I didn't get to savor it, there was too much junk in the way."

"The old 'You'll ruin your dinner' bit. I've heard that plenty of times."

Swap took the barber's cloth off the boy and the kid jumped off the chair. His dad sent him to the bathroom to clean up and told him to play with Slobber in the back. Then he said, "You guys don't mind if I stick around do you?"

"Not at all," Swap said.

"We all heard the 'You'll ruin your dinner' speech," Tom said, "and it doesn't really matter when you're a kid hungry for candy and your mom is trying to reason with vegetable soup. But when you know the meal is something special, like my New York strips, you can say no to the Gummy Bears.

J, I spend a lot of time mentoring and counseling young married couples and almost every one of them carries a sexual history into their marriage. You've grown up in a time where marriage is marginalized and multiple sexual experi-

SEASONS

ences are elevated, and I'm telling you the multiple experiences myth is Gummy Bears – a mirage of fulfillment followed by lingering consequences."

"I've heard this one too."

"Okay, fine, but hear me out. When most young people hear this kind of thing they tune out because they don't believe marriage, and particularly sex within a marriage, is all that special, and on top of that they're convinced sexual experimentation is the pot of gold. But J, to shift gears just a little bit, would you listen to one of your high school or college friends tell you the NFL was no big deal?"

"I'd listen, but I'd ignore them."

"What if they asked you to skip a workout or violate a team rule, citing how silly it is that you would try for the NFL considering how few make it as their reasoning?"

"I might reconsider being their friend."

"Because you've allowed yourself to get a full picture of what being in the NFL will mean to you and your family. You imagine the exhilaration of living the dream. You picture the financial security living that dream provides. You know throwing that away for some momentary pleasure would be plain old dumb."

"More than dumb, bordering on criminal."

"J, if you would just listen to someone who's in the league, so to speak, the momentary pleasure mirage that is premarital sex is the same kind of dumb. A strong marriage is far more valuable than a few years in the NFL, and nothing does more to erode your chances at a strong marriage than premarital

OPPORTUNITIES

sex. People overcome it all the time; that's what people like me help couples do. But helping couples get to true marital health after premarital sexual experiences is like watching the coaches get *The Biggest Loser* contestants in shape. It's stressful, painful, emotionally exhausting work."

"Well, that's a picture I've never been given during a sex talk."

"This isn't a sex talk. This is about you knowing what's good and being ready to thrive when your opportunity comes, and knowing what's not good and being ready to run when those opportunities come. The principle applies to football, marriage, education, whatever. The problem comes when we let ourselves get distracted by the moment and lose sight of our future goals."

"I've never really thought about things other than my football goals in that way, but I can see that I should start."

"Well, if you don't, instead of looking forward with hope, you'll be left looking back with regret."

The man paid for his son's haircut and thanked Swap. Then he turned to Tom, "I appreciate you letting me listen in on your conversation. It was a good reminder for me." He shook Tom's hand, then yelled for his son, "Let's go Ben, mom's gonna have dinner waiting on us." The little boy ran through Swap's Shop with Slobber chasing behind, wagging his nubby tail.

"I better be going myself, 'Happy wife, happy life' right?" Mr. Cothran stood. I stood as well.

SEASONS

"I really appreciate you coming by today, Tom," Swap said, shaking Mr. Cothran's hand.

"I enjoyed it, Swap. I always enjoy coming by your shop. Maybe next time I'll actually get my hair cut."

"If you do, it's on me," my grandpa said.

"Mr. Cothan, thanks for talking with me," I said.

"It was an honor, J. There was a guy who did the same for me one day many years ago." He nodded over at Swap as he said it, "and I'm glad to return the favor. Jeff, we'll see you later, hopefully after you've napped."

"Yeah, yeah," Jeff said, "See you around, Tom."

After walking out the door, Mr. Cothran stuck his head back inside, "And Jeff, you may want to consider going through that stack of magazines. I think you'll find what you've been looking for." He winked at me and I smiled. Jeff looked at him like he'd just said he had a pet leprechaun. Swap shook his head and laughed.

DISCUSSION QUESTIONS

1. Mr. Cothran said he wanted his athletic goals to transcend the game and settled on three that would help him both on and off the field: "having the best attitude possible, working harder each day than he had before, and being absolutely dependable." What do you think about those goals? Do you think they would've harder or easier to achieve than something like a goal of becoming an All-American?

2. Why might goals that have to do with playing time or statistics tempt you to give up? What can you do to avoid that trap? Would you say it's bad to have statistical goals or All-American types of goals? Why or why not?

3. You read how you have to know where you want to go, but also where you don't want to go; you have to have a line you won't cross. Performance Enhancing Drugs were used as an example of this principle. What are your thoughts on this two-pronged approach to your future? What are some goals that might tempt you to cross a line? What are some good lines to establish? What are some examples of goals you could set that would help you steer clear of lines?

SEASONS

4. Golfers do a great job of anticipating bad scenarios, such as balls in the bunker or behind trees, and they prepare mentally and physically for those situations if they should happen in live play. How important do you think it is to mentally prepare yourself for bad opportunities you may see in life? What are some things you can do to anticipate and prepare for bad opportunities?

5. Mr. Stanley said many of our problems come from when we "get distracted by the moment and lose sight of our future goals." Why do you think that's true? What can you do to avoid those distractions? What are some goals that are compelling enough that you would be less tempted by momentary distractions?

—chapter twelve—

INTEGRITY

DOES YOUR LIFE LINE UP?

What you are as a person is far more important that what you are as a basketball player.
—JOHN WOODEN,
2006 College Basketball Hall of Fame inductee

"J," SWAP SAID, "this last conversation will be a little different."

"How so?"

"Mostly because Jeff and I are leaving you alone for this one."

"Okay. But why, what's going on?"

"You'll be fine, you actually know this last visitor pretty well."

Jeff was already finished cleaning around his chair and gathering all his stuff. Swap didn't have much to gather considering he left his wallet on his seat and his keys may have been out there too. He called for Slobber and the three of them headed for the door.

"Don't worry about locking up. I'll either come back tonight or get it in the morning," Swap said.

"Uh, Grandpa, I think coming back tonight would be the thing to do."

"You are always worrying about stuff getting stolen. Believe it or not, burglars aren't spending their time stalking old barbers and devising strategies to steal hair scissors."

"In this case I'm not so much concerned about your store as much as I am your family, me in particular."

"You want me to lock you in here? What are you so afraid of?"

"No, I don't want to be locked in. I want a ride home."

He grinned. "Don't you worry about that, just trust old Swap." He winked at me, got in his truck with Slobber and rumbled down the road. So there I sat, thoughts of what I'd been hearing today blending with curiosity about what was still to come and my mind swirled. I couldn't imagine what

INTEGRITY

else there was to talk about and I was clueless as to who might walk through the door. I figured getting my body to mirror my mind might help so I climbed into one of the barber chairs and tried to see how many rotations I could turn on one push. I'd gotten up to five when I heard the bell over the door ring. My back was turned, so I spun the chair one hundred eighty degrees to see who had come in. Swap wasn't joking. I knew this man very well.

"Hi, Dad."

"Hey, J. How many spins did you get?"

"Five, but how did you know that's what I was doing?"

"As a man who's done his share of chair spinning, I knew exactly what was going on."

My dad and I got along pretty well; my friends thought he was great. My mom says I look just like he did when they met and I'd be lying if I told you it didn't creep me out just a little. He was a firefighter, so he had one of those twenty-four hours on, forty-eight hours off schedules which was pretty cool during my senior year. I'd bet there were at least five times he let me skip school so we could spend a day on our boat. That's the kind of thing that made my friends think he was so great. Ever since I was little he'd done things like that. He once showed up on a Monday when I was in second grade with a Mickey Mouse balloon and told me and the whole lunch room I was leaving right then to spend a week at Disney World. That might have been the coolest thing he's ever done. He was a college athlete, too, having wrestled for a small school in the Midwest. He was in the weight class just below the heavyweights and won two national championships. There was one year between his graduation and the Olympic trials and he says that's what cost him; he lost by one point to the guy who eventually won bronze. He was done with wrestling after that and has been fighting fires ever since.

"So you're my last guest, huh?"

"That's right. I thought it would be best this way." The chair next to me squeaked when he sat down. Then he spun it to face me.

"Wait, you set all this up? I thought Grandpa did it."

"We were co-conspirators. He did something similar for me before I went to college, so I asked him to help me do it for you. How's it been?"

"It's actually been good. Grandpa knows some pretty cool people."

"That's the truth; he knows everybody. If I would have been in charge, you would have been talking to me, Jeff, and a few guys at the station, but certainly not big shots like Jackson James. Dad went above and beyond for you, J."

"Well, it's been good. I'm glad he did it, and you did it."

"I know you've heard some of this stuff before, but I also know from experience sometimes hearing things from someone other than your dad helps it sink in."

"You know from experience?"

"Yeah. There was stuff my dad told me over and over again that I didn't really pay attention to, but when my wrestling coach in college said them I ate it up. I don't know why it

INTEGRITY

happens, but it seems pretty common."

"Maybe if you started an expedition service into the Amazon, I'd listen better."

He laughed. "I'll see what I can do."

"So what's your topic? I feel like everything's been covered."

"You have covered a lot, and what I have to talk about touches almost all of it. We're going to talk about character, J."

"Character is what you do when no one else is watching. I can't think of a day when we didn't talk about character," I said.

He laughed again. "I know, that's because it's so important. But I want you to really think about it today."

"Haven't you wanted me to think about it every time we've talked about it?"

"Of course, but I've been thinking more about it and realized I haven't been very clear about what good character is. We've talked about having character and living with character, but left it at that. But what makes one person's character good and another's bad? Are there some things you should do and some you shouldn't? Stuff like that."

"I guess you're right. I've assumed you were basically telling me to tell the truth and do the right thing, but maybe it's something else. I haven't really thought about it beyond that."

"Here's a thought. Character's supposed to be about what you do when no one's watching; doing the right thing if you knew you would get away with doing wrong. But when you think about it, your character is almost always talked about in how others perceive you, isn't it?"

"How do you mean?"

"If you were arrested for something, your attorney might have people come and testify on your behalf and they are called character witnesses. But if character is all about what you do when no one's watching, what is a character witness going to talk about?"

"They would tell the judge if you're a good guy or not, or if you tell the truth, I guess."

"Yeah, but there have been plenty of criminals who convinced people they were good guys, but they were people who completely lacked character."

"That's true. But maybe that just undercuts the idea of a character witness and doesn't have anything to do with a person's character at all."

"And I think you're right about that," Dad said. "But if that's true, how in the world do we know if we have good character? What's our standard?"

I started to speak but stopped when I realized I didn't have any idea what the answer to his question was. I thought about it for a minute and finally spoke, "I don't know. I just thought it meant to tell the truth."

"This is kind of where I got stuck too. So I started to think about it from the perspective of evaluating whether or not someone else has character and came down to a question: Can I trust the person?"

"I'd probably say the same thing," I said.

"But the problem is, I only have my eye witness account or the eye witness testimony of a reference to go on, and as we've established, people can be great actors with poor character."

INTEGRITY

"That's really all you'd ever have to go on though, isn't it?"

"The more I thought about it, the more I came to realize character assumes you and the person in question agree on what is and isn't good. You and I, for example, probably know what the other person means when they say 'character,' but what about someone who wasn't raised in our home? Would their definition be different?"

"I wouldn't think so. Wouldn't something like lying reveal poor character all the time?"

"Maybe, but we mostly think about lying as something someone says."

"That's basically what lying is, saying something that isn't true."

"But then I got to thinking about the family that hid Anne Frank and her family from the Nazis, and the people who organized the Underground Railroad. No doubt, they said many things that weren't true, but I would say in both instances they were doing the right thing. Wouldn't you?"

"I guess I would. Well, now I'm confused."

"Sometimes getting lost is the only way to learn if you really knew where you were going to begin with."

"What?"

"Never mind. What helped me was when I stopped thinking about truth and lies in relation to what a person says and started thinking about it in relation to whether or not a person's life lines up, or runs parallel, to truth."

I scrunched my face and raised my left eyebrow. "You're gonna have to give me a little more."

SEASONS

"If that family told a Nazi guard they knew nothing about the Franks, we'd say they both told a lie yet did the right thing, right?"

"Right," I said.

"So there's something deeper we're thinking about, something more beautiful than what we say."

"Yeah I guess, but what?"

"I found thinking about it from the other angle helped. What if the guy told the truth and the Franks were murdered? He told the truth, but what would you say about him?"

"I'd probably call him a coward, maybe worse."

"But would you trust him?"

"You know," I paused. "I don't think so."

"And why?"

"He told the truth, but telling the truth was just convenient. Frankly, it was selfish in that moment, cruel even. I don't think I could trust a guy who was out for himself like that."

"That was my thought exactly. But if you had a friend who stole something and you knew about it, and then a cop asked you about it, would you be doing the right thing to lie about it?"

"Yeah, well, no. I don't know."

"I think you do."

"No then. I think the right thing to do there would be to tell the truth. But it would be hard."

"And that was a clue to me about character. Sure, it's doing the right thing when no one's watching, but it's also doing the right thing when everyone's watching and doing it is hard or

INTEGRITY

unpopular. It's tied to courage and sacrifice; it can't be motivated by protecting yourself."

"I think I'd agree with that," I said.

"I even think there are times when a person's actions can be wrong and they reveal him to be a person of great character."

"Like when?"

"I don't know. Imagine a surly, angry, bad dude wearing a cop uniform, and then imagine a frail, starving child."

"Okay."

"What if you saw the little boy steal an apple, the store owner noticing the apple was gone and telling Officer Jerk. With rage in his eyes, you saw the bully cop approach the boy so you decide to intervene by leaning your shoulder into him as he passes and knock the cop down. I'd say you showed good character, but also poor judgment at the same time. A person develops good judgment as they experience new things, make mistakes, and do things correctly. But good character can be present throughout, regardless of someone's age."

"You're saying just because somebody does something stupid or makes a mistake doesn't necessarily mean they are people of poor character. Is that right?"

"Yeah. Being young can make you do stupid things, but it doesn't always reveal a lack of character."

"So what is it then? You said it was something about a person's life lining up with truth. What were you talking about?"

"I think good character has to come from somewhere. It doesn't change over time, or from person to person, or place to place."

SEASONS

"Meaning what?"

"Meaning you can't be a guy who just tells the truth. You have to have some sort of code you submit to, a transcendent set of principles that influence your decision making. For example, I would be less concerned with *if* you told the truth and more concerned with *why* you told the truth. If your life goal was to become wealthy, you might tell the truth when it moved you toward that goal but just as easily lie if it moved you in the same direction. I want people in my life who would tell the cops if I stole something and also tell the Gestapo they didn't know where I was."

"Okay, but that example doesn't totally help me because it only tells me something I shouldn't be motivated by. If character comes from somewhere, then where?"

"My coach in college was a man of outstanding character. Thinking back, I realized the only reason I knew was because he regularly told us his priorities and they gave us the measuring stick to evaluate who he was. We could tell if what he professed lined up with what he actually did."

"So I just need to have priorities and then tell people about them?"

"Sort of. But it also matters what those priorities are. No matter what a man's priorities are, you can at least tell if he is who he claims to be by seeing if his actions line up with his priorities. He may be about getting rich, buying toys, and easy living, and he may spend his time researching, buying, and selling real estate, driving fancy cars, and having hired

INTEGRITY

help clean his house; you may not think he's got proper priorities but at least he's consistent. See what I mean?"

"Yeah. But would you trust that guy?"

"Nope, and it's because of his priorities. He'd turn on me in a blink if the money was right."

"Then why are we talking about him?"

"He was just an example, don't worry about him. My college coach professed his priorities like this, 'My Lord, my lady, my legacy, and my learning,' and he lived like he meant them. He wouldn't say it exactly like this, but he believed God provided us with that transcendent set of ideas and principles to direct our lives, so his primary goal was to know God and live a life to honor him. As a married man, he believed his 'lady' took priority over everything in his life except God. When he said his legacy, he was talking about his kids and grandkids and being a mentor for the guys he coached. And finally, he believed people should always be learning something and be intentional about it."

"Then if I'm going to be a man of character I have to have those same priorities?"

"Not necessarily, but very close. You aren't married, so to put your lady at number two would mess your life up. If you asked me, I'd tell you your family is number two and as your role within the family changes, that priority gets more specific."

"What do you mean?"

"Right now, your responsibility is to honor and obey me and your mom. Therefore, it should be your number two priority. When you go off to college, obeying us will be less impactful because you won't have us in your home, so honor should become the primary goal between those two. If a girl becomes a part of your life, then she has to begin moving up your list until she becomes number two or your relationship ends. But, and we've talked about this before, if a girl comes into your life, I absolutely expect you to place honoring her parents at number three on your list. family is up there, but it morphs as you grow up."

"That makes sense and all, but why? Why is that how it should be?"

"That goes back to the number one priority. Your number one has to be the singular influence for all the others. It's that transcendent set of principles—"

"Hold on. Was transcendent in your crossword this morning or something? You've said it about a dozen times and I'm not sure I know what it means."

My dad grinned. "I didn't even see the crossword this morning. Your mom had it in the bottom of your brother's rabbit cage before I had the chance. I hate that rabbit." He shook his head and we both laughed. "But transcendent just means something that lives beyond the current circumstances or time. You might say Beethoven's music was transcendent because people are still listening to it today, hundreds of years after he died. So transcendent principles are ideas that were relevant and true a long time ago, still are today, and will be for years to come."

"And you're saying God provided those ideas?"

"You know I believe that."

INTEGRITY

"Yeah I know, but we're talking about something else now. I know a lot of people – a lot – who say they don't believe in God or believe in some other god and I think I hear you telling me that would mean they couldn't be people of character because of it."

"That's not exactly what I'm saying. If you had a friend who professed a Jewish faith, you would be able to consider the Ten Commandments, for example, and expect him to live by that. How he lived in relation to those transcendent principles would help you evaluate what kind of character he had. He may not share your faith, but he could absolutely be a man of outstanding character. If you had a friend who said they were an atheist you'd have to really dig to find out what primary idea fueled all their other ideas. It would be far harder to truly evaluate what kind of man or woman they were."

"But why? I understand what you said about the Ten Commandments, but why do you say it would be so hard to know about the atheist?"

"Because the principles that guide your life and the principles that guide his are so different, to the point of being in opposition. And without knowing why he does what he does, you cannot be confident he will do the same things tomorrow. Let's say you were married and your wife's best friend was married to this hypothetical atheist."

"Am I married to someone cool?"

"Sure. Your wife was Miss Texas, won the Nobel Peace Prize in college, started her own company in high school and sold it before you married for two hundred million dollars.

She's a bigger football fan than you are, loves God, and prefers dogs to cats. Will that work?"

"Can she cook?"

"Not a lick. In fact she's offended you would even ask the question. But her two hundred million allows you to hire a chef who's a cooking phenomenon."

"Alright, I'll take that. You can go on."

"So her best friend—"

"Wait. What's her name?"

"I don't know." He was clearly annoyed, but I was having fun messing with him. "I'll call her Figment, because she doesn't exist."

"No way am I asking out a girl named Figment."

"Call her whatever you want, but I'm not talking about her name anymore. Anyway, her best friend is married to the atheist and one day the friend shows up sobbing because atheist man filed for divorce claiming to have found someone better looking than his wife. What do you do?"

"I guess I'd go talk to him."

"And say what?"

"That he was being selfish."

"But his personal happiness might be his number one priority and your claims of selfishness are meaningless to him."

"Then I would remind him of his vows and call him a liar."

"Again, so what. His vows are less important than his number one. If lying is necessary for his happiness, then lying it is."

"Then I would hit him for being stupid."

INTEGRITY

"Hold on there, tiger." He laughed. "He's being consistent."

"But he's being a jerk."

"And this is why it's hard. In this particular example, he lacks any transcendent values because his priority is happiness, and that lives and dies with him, and changes day to day. You're frustrated because you believe his behavior violates a code, while he believes there is no code to violate. And if you show me a man with no code, I'll show you a man with no character."

"Would you say the same about a man who claims a code, but the code is shady?"

"Absolutely. He may be consistent, like the guy earlier, and you might be able to anticipate his behavior, but I doubt he'd be a man of character, at least not how you or I would define it."

"So it's all about someone's first priority?"

"Kind of, but not exactly. It's ultimately about where a person gets their value system, and their first priority shows you both their value system and where it comes from."

"Do I just pick a first priority then?"

"If that's how you decided, what would be the source of your value system?"

"I guess I would be."

"One thing I know for sure, being the source of your own value system isn't going to work."

"Then what do I do?"

"I told you where I get mine. You have to figure out where you get yours and prioritize your life accordingly. No one can

SEASONS

do that for you. Maybe think of a few people you know and admire, and ask them where their value system comes from. Maybe grab a biography of a person from history you think possessed quality character and see what motivated him. In the meantime, you may want to adopt, or copy, the values held by me or your grandpa and see how they work for you, because the world won't stop spinning while you figure it all out."

"'My Lord, my lady, my legacy, and my learning.' That's what your coach said, right?"

"That was it. And I simply tweaked the lady part to family because I wasn't married at the time. However, I did strive to live with my future lady in mind. Meaning I worked to honor her even before we met."

"How does that look now, since mom passed and you have a new lady?"

"That's a great question, J. The truth is there's no shame in my relationship with your mom. Mary knew all about your mom from the first time we met and she has always been supportive. She's never felt as if there was some sort of competition and has always encouraged me to remember and honor your mom's legacy. I believe I am able to honor your mom and honor Mary without the two ever being in conflict. Had my time with your mother been littered with regret or shame it might have been harder, but it wasn't. Believe it or not, the fact that I honored my marriage to your mom with such resolve makes Mary even more confident in our marriage, because she knows my motivation isn't based on circumstance."

INTEGRITY

"Because you did things right the first time, she's confident you'll do things right this time too?"

"And she knows my values are rooted in something transcendent, something outside the bounds of circumstance and time. Speaking of time, what time is it?"

I grabbed my phone. "5:45, why?"

"Because I promised Mary we'd be home by six o'clock. We've got to leave now or she's gonna kill me."

"Fine with me," I said. "I'm starving."

I heard the bell ring a final time as the door closed behind us. As soon as we were on the sidewalk, I noticed there were no cars parked in front of the store. "Where did you park?"

"I didn't."

"Then how did you get here?"

"One of the guys from the station dropped me off on his way in."

"Then how are we getting home?"

"You're driving."

"I caught a ride with Grandpa, and as you can see," I waved my hand toward the street, "I have no car here either."

"Hmm, that is a problem." He tried to play cool, but had a terrible poker face. Over his shoulder, I saw Swap's truck roll to a stop a few blocks up the road. Slobber was in his regular spot, but Jeff was in the driver's seat. He pulled out and took a left to drive toward us. Then Swap pulled up to the stop sign in a car I hadn't seen before. It was a yellow and white jeep-looking vehicle that looked rugged but well taken care of. Swap turned our direction and my dad's grin got even bigger. Jeff parked and leaned out the driver's window, then Swap pulled in and stepped out, leaving the car running.

"J," my dad said, "you remember your conversation with the Stanfords, right?"

"Yeah, of course." As soon as he said their name I remembered the story about this car.

"This was their son, Paul's, Land Cruiser, but now it's yours." My grandpa stepped away from the door and held his arm out to usher me into the driver's seat.

"Mine, like, to have?"

"Yes, son. Yours to have. We figured you would need something reliable to get to school and back so your grandfather and I bought it for you. What do you think?"

I stared at my dad, who still had a goofy grin, only now I had the same one on my face. "You're serious? This is mine?"

He nodded, "Yep."

"And I get to take it to college?"

"Yep."

"By myself?"

He laughed, "Well, we sure aren't going to drive you around, but Mary might want to come along."

I half skipped, half ran to the driver's seat and sat down behind the wheel. I knew it wasn't new, but it felt like it. Swap slowly closed the door and he and my dad stood outside the window. I looked out the front, gripped the steering wheel, and imagined driving.

"You remember the story behind this car don't you son?" Dad's smile was gone, but he wasn't upset.

INTEGRITY

"Yes sir, I remember."

"J," Swap finally spoke up, "every time you get in this car I want you to remember how you came to be the one driving it and why Paul Stanford isn't anymore. Remember what you heard today."

"I will, Grandpa, every time." And I meant it.

"I love you, J, and I'm proud of you," he said. "You deserve this, but not because you can play football. You deserve it because you're a fine young man and you honor your family in how you live."

"Thanks, Grandpa. Thanks for everything."

He squeezed my shoulder, "You're welcome, J." He started to walk away.

"Wait." I opened the door, hopped out of my seat, jogged up to him, and gave him a hug. "I love you, Grandpa." He hugged me back, "I love you too, J." We let go of each other and I got back in my car while he walked around the front of my new Land Cruiser, kicked Jeff out of his truck's driver's seat, and sat down next to Slobber.

My dad was waiting in the passenger seat next to me. "You ready to go home?"

"Yes, sir!" As I reached to put it in gear my phone vibrated. I looked at the text and read it out loud, *"Don't let your fancy new car cause you to forget your mom. I still need you to pick up some milk! See you when you get home. Love you more…"*

"You better tell her we'll be late," my dad said.

"Leaving Swap's Shop now. Stopping at the store on the way. We're gonna be L8 & it's dad's fault." I read that out loud too.

SEASONS

"Nice, J. I appreciate you being a team player."

"Hey, I've gotta tell the truth, even if the truth gets you in trouble, and especially if it means Mom might give me your dessert."

Dad just smiled, already lost in thought, and my smile matched his. It had been a good day.

DISCUSSION QUESTIONS

1. How would you have defined "having good character" before you read this chapter? Has your definition changed at all? How would you define it now?

2. What do you think about the idea that telling truth and telling a lie are bigger than just what we say? Do you think the family who lied to the Nazi guards did the right thing, even if they told a lie? If so, do you then think any lie is fair game? Why or why not?

3. J's dad said character included "doing the right thing when everyone is watching, and doing it is hard or unpopular. It's tied to courage and sacrifice; it can't be motivated by protecting yourself." What do you think about those ideas? Have you ever had to do the right thing when it was unpopular?

4. Do you agree with Mr. Foxe's statement, "Being young can make you do stupid things, but it doesn't always reveal a lack of character"? Think back on the example with the frail kid, the mean cop, and J bumping the cop, what are some ways J could have intervened that would have displayed good character without using poor judgment?

SEASONS

5. What do you think about the coach's priority system: "My Lord, my lady (family), my legacy, and my learning"? Would you add or remove any from his list? Talk about the relationship between a person's stated priorities and evaluating their character?

THE BENCH

In a park on a summer day
An old man sits watching children play.
They run and slide, they jump and climb.
They've no concern for the hands of time.
His mind goes back to younger years
When he played The Game and people cheered.
Memories that once dormant lay
Come to him on The Bench that day.

A little boy with a hopeful dream
Imagined himself being on a team.
He knew for sure why he was born –
The ball, the game, the uniform.
Even if he'd never take the field,
He'd beam with pride on The Bench of steel.
He'd chase his goal, never losing steam;
The Game became his life's new theme.

SEASONS

His soccer mom took him to the field
With halftime oranges that the players peeled.
When the soccer season's time was done
He changed his shoes for the coming one.
He raced in pools, dribbled on the court;
Whatever the season, he played the sport.
One day he knew other sports must yield.
He chose The Game, his heart was sealed.

On all-star teams, then travel ball;
To be the best, he gave his all.
The first one there, the last to leave,
He'd be the best, he would achieve.
With skill and heart — tools of the trade —
He found success no matter where he played.
Until he walked those high school halls
And spent a season on The Bench that fall.

The Bench now cruel — a seat of shame —
Reserved for those kept from The Game.
He worked real hard and pushed through fear;
He joined The Game the coming year.
Freed from The Bench, his world was right,
He played with skill, with grace, with might.
And to no surprise, recruiters came.
He chose a school. The dream his aim.

THE BENCH

On campus now, the season begins,
But he finds himself on The Bench again.
Try as he might, it takes two years
Before he plays and hears the cheers.
But once he does, he grows in fame —
From on The Bench to household name.
He finished well and was ready when
The big leagues called — the dream begins.

Getting there was just the start;
He had big goals, he'd leave his mark.
So he gave his all, he persevered,
But found himself on The Bench for years.
'Till one day Coach called him aside,
"I'm sorry, son, your dream has died."
He played no more, but stayed with The Game
Back on The Bench, now "Coach" his name.

It broke his heart to leave the field,
but eventually those cracks would heal.
He found his will and drive again;
The Bench became his trusted friend.
And over the years The Bench did grow
Into his pulpit, shop, and studio.
But after decades on The Bench had passed,
He was forced to leave his seat at last.

SEASONS

He'd been so focused on The Dream —
The Bench, The Game, being on the team -
That he somehow missed along the way
Those closest to him and the price *they* paid.
His wife had raised their son alone.
He'd missed so much; he should have known.
Freed from The Bench he'd held so tight,
He'd find a way to make things right.

He began to date his lovely bride.
She asked to dance and so he tried.
With his son there were miles to walk,
So he called him up and they began to talk.
His son forgave him but made a plea,
"Be the best grandfather that you can be!"
So he'd take those kids for a walk outside,
and find a bench close to the slides.

In a park on a summer day
An old man sits watching children play.

ABOUT THE AUTHOR

RYAN SPRAGUE

After winning a national championship on the 1999 Florida State Seminoles' football team, Ryan began competing in the real world. God used his decade as a pastor to nurture his passion for helping families. Now, with more than ten years of marriage, four young sons and a beloved daughter, Ryan is even more enthusiastic about partnering with families as they fight for their homes. He lives with his family in Tallahassee, Florida and whether it's a book, a blog post, an article, or delivering a talk, Ryan strives to present life changing truth in a clear, creative way. Words are powerful.

> *"And because of His words many more became believers."*
> – JOHN 4:41

SEASONS

Ryan has spoken in elementary, middle, and high schools, to college groups, professional groups, church groups, and entire churches. If you're interested in inviting Ryan to come speak to your group, please contact him through one of the following ways.

You can reach Ryan by visiting his website:
www.ryansprague.com

Or connecting on Facebook:
www.facebook.com/ryanspraguegrateful

OTHER BOOKS BY RYAN SPRAGUE

Nonfiction
*Grateful: From Walking on
to Winning it all at Florida State*

For Children
The Unconquered Chronicles (e-book)
The Magic Ticket (e-book)

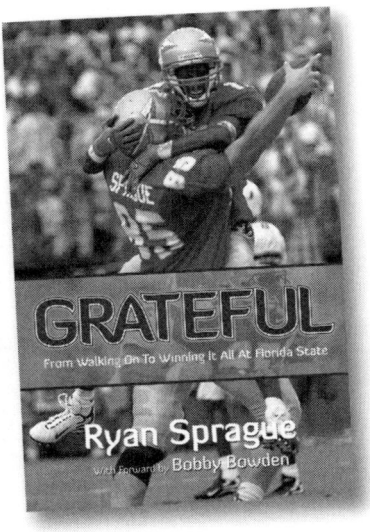

GRATEFUL
From Walking on to Winning it All at Florida State

by Ryan Sprague

Grateful is available at Barnes & Noble, Garnet & Gold, Bill's Bookstore, Alumni Hall, and The Florida State University Bookstore.

www.ryansprague.com

Have you ever wondered what it would be like to **win a National Championship?**

Do you **root for the underdogs?**

We all know **the stars**, but are you one who wants to know about the **unsung heroes?**

Would you want to be a **fly on the wall** when a **living legend speaks?**

In *Grateful,* you'll get that chance. You'll get a personal perspective of the legendary Bobby Bowden, a refreshing look at one history's great football dynasties, and a glimpse into the unfamiliar, family side of Florida State football.

> "Sprague takes us inside one of the great programs in college football history and tells the story of a coaching icon as only a former player can. There is the joy and laughter that winners feel. But there are also sadness and tears, especially when the great man has to leave the stage. Ryan Sprague knows that both are necessary to tell the story. And he tells it very well"
>
> – TONY BARNHART, CBS Sports

SHOP IN LOVE AT CYNY.ORG

15% OFF CODE: "J4H7B85"

Clothe Your Neighbor as Yourself is a non-profit clothing brand built on the simple idea that **for every clothing item you purchase, you help provide clothing to someone in need**. It all started in 2009 when our founder sold everything to go live with the homeless.

Buy a shirt, we give a school uniform to an orphan in Africa. **Buy a hat**, we give a wig to someone battling cancer. **Buy a bag**, we give a backpack to a child in poverty. **Buy a hoodie or scarf**, we give a warm coat to a homeless friend. The list goes on...

FOLLOW US & OUR FOUNDER

@CYNYORG & @JAMESTHEVERB